The Profit SECRET

How to sell more at a higher margin

Nick Baldock and Bob Hayward

The Profit Secret

First published in 2020 by

Panoma Press Ltd
48 St Vincent Drive, St Albans, Herts, AL1 5SJ, UK
info@panomapress.com
www.panomapress.com

Book layout by Neil Coe.
Illustrations by Craig Thomas.

978-1-784529-11-6

Dedication

For Nick

On Sunday 13th July 2014 I got a call from Kirsty, the wife of my best friend, running buddy, co-author and business partner Nick Baldock, telling me he had died of a sudden heart attack. They had been married for 12 years; Nick had a daughter, Lauren. I know the impact on their lives and mine cannot be compared – and yet… Such a big part of my life simply disappeared. No time to say goodbye. No time to plan and adjust. There one day and gone the next.

The death of a loved one can be devastating; whether friend or family, whether a life partner or a business partner. As friend and business partner I was devastated. That week I called all the clients Nick was working with at that time, I was stunned by some reactions. While all were upset and sympathetic, I could hear some of the apparent hardnosed sales directors in tears on the phone – such was Nick's impact on people.

That impact was, and is, huge. His runs the length of the UK (one for the British Heart Foundation, one for burns victim Arthur Page), Death Valley, various islands and the Forest Gump across America for Josie Russell, inspired people and raised a lot of money for charity. His training and consultancy turned careers, teams and businesses around. His encyclopaedic knowledge and faultless re-enactment of Monty Python, Tommy Cooper and The Two Ronnies as well as countless other comedy acts are still making people smile and laugh today. I can still hear him saying "No one expects the Spanish Inquisition!"

Even as I write these words in 2020, Nick's teaching and jokes pop into my thoughts daily. Clients still quote him, "Bob, do you remember what Nick used to say?" Yes, I do. And so do they. His wisdom, presence and encouragement are still impacting people. Still helping people challenge and improve. Still making people smile and laugh.

Nick and I had almost finished the second book, *Persuade*, when he died. While I was desperate to finish the book to honour Nick, I could not even look at the book for two years. I struggled emotionally with the final edit for two more years and finally published it in 2018. *Persuade* was an immediate success and continues to sell well. This book, *The Profit Secret*, has been a similar struggle for me emotionally. Even though this is a business book Nick's words are on every page, and while for you they may be simply pure inspiration, for me they also remind me how much I miss him. Completing both books has been a cathartic experience for me, as well as a labour of love.

I know now that my life is not better without Nick, it is better because of him. It is richer because of him. It is brighter because of him. Even now I can hear him singing *"Always look on the bright side of life…"* to encourage us all.

Testimonials

"No matter what business you're in, a crucial aspect of your business is sales and this book will help you to sell more, more often, and at a better price. The authors directly and brilliantly tackle the timeless challenge that anyone and everyone in business faces – being asked to drop the price. Read this book and save yourself from years of headaches and lost revenue that can too often result from stressful, back-and-forth, price-negotiation situations."

**Dr Ivan Misner, NY Times Bestselling Author,
CEO and Founder of BNI, the largest
business networking club**

"The authors have put together in this book an essential toolkit for anyone in sales and negotiations, this is a must read."

**Jim Hetherton, VP International Operations,
On Track International**

"The business that can define and develop its value chain will be the one that will survive the economic difficulties. This book is a toolkit that will give any sales team the knowledge and skills on how to present a professional proposition. The process steps are simple, logical – based on practical experience and best of all – they work!"

**Will Doherty, Training Specialist DNATA
Emirates Airlines**

"The authors have a gem of a book. Super, highly practical advice that when followed will close more sales and generate a stack of repeat business."

Richard Denny, Author of *Selling to Win*

Described by *The Times* newspaper as "The master of professional salesmanship".

"Your ability to sell higher priced products against lower priced competition is the key to more sales and higher income – and the book shows you how to do it."

Brian Tracy, Author of *The Psychology of Selling*

"This book is a great tool for any businesses that are looking to defend their margins."

James Caan, BBC's *Dragons' Den*

"The best book I've read on sales – directly tackling a problem for many businesses, being asked to drop the price. Whatever you sell, this book will save you a fortune by reducing the number and amount of discounts you would have given away."

Thomas Power, Business is Personal

Contents

Dedication   3

Testimonials   5

Contents   7

Introducing the Profit Secret   9

Chapter 1   Sales are vanity; profit is sanity   13

Chapter 2   Building a sales proposition is
            like building a house   25

Chapter 3   Where to build your business
            profitably   35

Chapter 4   Digging the foundations of profit
            and value   49

Chapter 5   Laying the cornerstones of profit   67

Chapter 6   Laying the final cornerstone
            of profit   91

Chapter 7   The framework of profit, the tools,
             systems and meetings   111

Chapter 8   The internal building blocks of profit   129

Chapter 9   The external building blocks of profit   153

Chapter 10   The roof: your sales conversation   173

Chapter 11   Resolve snags to keep more of
             the profit   207

Chapter 12   Keeping bad weather out: part one   221

Chapter 13   Keeping bad weather out: part two   235

Chapter 14   Future-proofing your profit   251

Chapter 15   Conclusion and Covid-19   269

Acknowledgements   275

About the authors   277

Introducing the Profit Secret

I do not claim that this book contains all the secrets of selling more at a higher margin, more often – just a lot of them. This book doesn't claim to have all the answers – what book does? I do not claim that this book is 100% full of brand-new ideas. Many have my own twists and many of those could be new to you. And while many of the origins of the ideas can be found in the public domain, right under every salesperson's nose, most are hidden – secret.

What I have sought to do is to combine some of the best thinking with my own ideas, to help consider how to ensure our businesses are profitable by building sales propositions based on value; our 'Value House'. In that respect, this book is a like a blended whisky rather than a single malt.

Much of the book is based on my own experiences and those of other salespeople I have interviewed – people of mixed age and ability. There are also several ideas from other books and from people who have contributed their own thoughts.

This book looks at what is probably the single biggest challenge businesses and salespeople face, which is price resistance, from a fresh perspective. Discounting too easily or too often and without a fair trade in terms of something back from the prospect will undermine your profitability.

The Profit Secret will help you if you are building a sales operation from scratch, by pointing you in the right direction for all the elements you may wish to consider. You will see as you go through the book that in many of the chapters an extra guide is available for download from my website, free, should you wish to do so. I recommend that you download the guides, some of which contain activities to help you get the most from this book.

If you are not building a sales operation from scratch and already run a business or are involved in a sales operation for an existing company, I hope this book encourages you to consider each element that we cover. Maybe you will examine how you are currently approaching that element. In the process of asking yourself, "What do we actually do in this area? What practice do we use?" you may consider blending in some ideas from this book. Even if you are happy with the way you currently do things, it is good to always challenge – even if we find out that what we do now IS best practice.

Today, selling is as much about the salesperson having intuition, an awareness of human behaviour and an appreciation of commercial politics as it is about sales process, tools and structure. To be successful, consistently, one needs to be able to demonstrate all these skills. Neglecting any one of these could upset a delicate balance. These days, prospects are more aware; they expect more and are more 'savvy'. Moreover, selling to some buyers has its fair share of games, tactics and to some extent trickery. Buyers may create this wonderful illusion through their body language, tone of voice and choice of words that unless we move on price, it is unlikely we will get the sale.

But as this book discusses, that may not always be the truth. As they say, all is fair in love and war. *The Profit Secret* shows how we can hold on to more of our margin and still win the sale.

My aim is to encourage the reader to consider three questions on our journey together through the book:

1. Do I do this?

2. To what extent is what I currently do successfully profitable?

3. If I could apply one aspect of the Profit Secret from each chapter, which one would improve my results the most?

It may well be, of course, that what you currently do enables you to achieve what you believe to be the maximum price, even under pressure, which is worthy of congratulations. Still, challenging ourselves frequently is a great idea, even when it sometimes proves that the way we are doing something IS the right way to do it – for now.

CHAPTER 1

Sales are vanity; profit is sanity

I remember it being very hot that day in Dallas in spring 1985.

For an Englishman in a suit and tie in 95°F heat, it was hot. The sun gleamed and glistened on the mirrored windows of the imposing convention centre as daily Dallas life bustled around it. Lanes of cars moved down freeways with purpose. I stood looking out of the mezzanine floor window at the traffic below, listening to the piped hotel music. It was *Missing you* by John Waites, *"Every time I think of you, I always catch my breath..."*

I was there to help the organisers running a sales seminar. The convention centre was big, bright and brash – or so it seemed to me at the time. I was on the door with someone else. Our job was to register people who had booked to attend the sales seminar and to sell tickets at $99.00 to anyone who hadn't booked but had turned up wanting to get in.

The seminar was due to start at 09.30 and at about 09.00 we were asked by the seminar organisers to sell tickets at half price for anyone who wanted to attend but hadn't booked. The person I was working with noticed someone near the reception area looking purposefully at the information we had put on display. The curious bystander picked up one leaflet, gave it a cursory glance and then picked up another and began to study it with some focus. He was about 30 and wore smart jeans with a crisp white shirt and casual shoes. He had the sort of tan that suggested he wasn't from England. I felt the cool air from the air conditioning blowing down on my head as my colleague drifted over to the bystander, no doubt hoping to sell him a half-price ticket.

"Hi there – how ya doin' today?" my colleague asked. "Would you like to attend today's seminar? You can pick up some great ideas and tips on better selling and how to influence people more," went his opening sales pitch. "Not only that, you'll be pleased to know that you can benefit from this action-packed day for only $49.99."

"Nah thanks, I'm not interested," the bystander replied, and turned with a polite smile.

"Sure thing – mind me asking why?" asked my colleague.

The young man replied, "Well, it's a lot of money."

My colleague left him at that, with a smile, thinking he would try and pitch to him again in another 10 minutes. So, when we were authorised to reduce the price even further and get people in to try and fill the remaining seats, he approached him again. "Hey buddy, you'll be pleased to know that I can now get you in for only $30 – what a great deal!"

The prospect looked at him momentarily, his eyes then drifting to one side before saying, "No – it's too expensive."

My colleague left, amazed that the other man thought that $30 was too expensive. He told me he was going to try one more time and went back after five minutes to say he could come in for $25, to which the young man replied it was still too expensive.

When the doors were closed, and it was too late anyway, my colleague asked him, "What about $5?" Not that he would have let him in at that price.

"No," came the answer again, and when asked why, the man said, "Well I'm just not that interested in attending."

What a massive lesson is in that answer! The fact that he didn't want to attend in the first place meant that **any** price would have been too high. The lesson is that unless a salesperson can establish two things first, there will almost always be price resistance. Those two things are: first, a genuine need or desire from the prospect; and second, the perception that the proposition contains greater relevant value than cost.

Those involved in selling – salespeople and businesses – often forget those two things and go chasing the sale at the expense of profit by reducing the price. Too often selling is vanity. Many forget that profit is sanity, not sales. It seems a secret that profit needs to be at the core of our approach to selling.

What is selling?

While there are various definitions my favourite is a secret – don't tell anyone:

> Selling is the process of enabling someone to discover something of relevant value to them, in a way that is profitable for us.

As we go through the book, we will examine how well this definition sits with selling on declared need and relevant value, how this helps you sell more at a higher margin, avoiding the price pressure and retaining the profit.

The way you define selling is the foundation on which all other aspects of the sales process are built. It does not matter how much you know about your company's products and services or how well you have memorised responses to every possible objection. What matters most is how you fundamentally define selling. And the above definition is the perfect foundation from which we can build robust approaches and strategies as well as a solid, sustainable and profitable business.

Remember, high-quality, ethical and profitable selling:

- is two way; it is impossible to sell unless you involve the person you are trying to sell to

- is a journey, not a destination

- is proactive, not reactive
- adds value to the buyer and profit to the seller

Good selling means it is the customer and not the product that comes back. Selling may be only the second oldest profession in the world but it is the highest paid. It is not always easy – it can be tough. After all, if it were easy, anyone would do it, right?

It's all about the price, isn't it?

The economic collapse in 2000–01 and the financial crisis of 2008 affected organisations and consumers in two key ways. Since then, trust has been more difficult to come by in business-to-business and business-to-consumer dealings; and in all parts of a business and in our lives, prices have come under increased scrutiny. In combination, these two things have led to buyers being more cautious and risk-averse, and buying processes and profits being squeezed. The Covid-19 pandemic in 2020 has added to this.

When people say to me, "Selling these days is all about the price," I say, "All things being equal, the sale will come down to price. Selling is about showing that things are not equal."

When the perceived relevant value of our proposition to the prospect is greater than the value of the money they hold and what the competition is offering, the prospect will happily trade their money for our proposition. They win. They get more out of the trade. The greater the difference between those two values, the easier the sale will be to secure and the more profitable our business will be.

This book is about meeting the challenge of price and the potential loss of profit head on. It is about how the sales operation in any business, especially your business, can be designed and built around those three key ingredients: the need, the value and the profit. Every sale you make can be built around those same three keys.

Many, if not most, sales are vanity. Making sales profitable must therefore be a secret, even though profit is sanity.

Why is profit a secret?

The concept of value being driven and measured by the customer rather than the seller seems to be accepted. Delivering true, relevant customer value is possible only by listening, asking, adapting, and changing as the world and customer needs change. Sales and marketing gurus and teams have become used to the concept of customer-centric value.

The concept of profit, however, is defined by the business or its owner. At its most basic level, profit is the margin gained by risk-taking entrepreneurs when the total revenue earned from selling a given output exceeds the total costs of producing and servicing that output.

If we increase the total revenue, we increase our total profits, provided we can hold the costs and protect our margin. Sometimes salespeople are tempted to reduce the price in the hope of achieving the sale. Of course, most buyers will ask for a discount. What happens if the salesperson gives even a 10% discount?

What is the true impact of giving any discount? Surely giving a 10% discount just means we need to sell 10% more product to make up for what we have given away, doesn't it?

The true cost of discounts

Say the regular selling price of an item in this store is £100. That item cost the retailer £60, so the gross profit is £40 or 40%. The retailer makes £0.40 as gross profit to pay wages and expenses on every £1.00 sold. When the salesperson gives a discount, the costs do not change; only the gross profit does.

With the 10% discount in the example above, the gross profit drops to £30, or 33.33%. Now only £0.33 of every £1.00 sold is available for wages and expenses.

In discovering the true costs of discounts, the business owner needs to ask, "How much more will I need in sales volume to generate the same amount of gross profit as before?"

The answer, the secret, is that instead of selling £100 to make £40, the salesperson must now sell £120.01 to make the same £40 in profit. That is a 20.01% increase in sales value. The business owner must now ask a variety of questions or risk losing money. These include:

- Will the market allow the store to sell at the full price? Is the discount necessary?

- Is there enough market demand to generate 20% more sales revenue because of the 10% drop in price?

- What additional operating costs will be incurred in providing 20% more sales to the marketplace?

- Can the company afford the 10% discount? Can it still be profitable at that lower price?

Profit is the secret that makes sales and business operate authentically. Profit has for too long been pushed aside in favour of a focus on customer-centric value. Forgotten by many at the sharp end of sales. You can deliver value to the market without profit if you wish, just not for very long. If you want your selling to be successful, for your business to succeed, you must make a profit.

There is, of course, another side to the Profit Secret. What happens when we increase the price? If the company raises the sales price in this example by 10%, the gross profit margin increases to 45.5%. Now the store is making 45.5% on every £1.00 and therefore needs to sell only £87.91 to make the same original £40 profit. That is a 12.09% decrease in volume. Ask any salesperson, "Would you rather have a 20% increase in your sales target or a 12% decrease for the same reward?"

"Hmmm let me think…"

Every sale you make, and every business, can be built around those same three keys: the need, the value and the profit. We know that building a house on sand or with the wrong materials is a daft idea, yet we often build sales propositions and businesses on weak, flaky ideas.

Sales are vanity; profit is sanity.

My original sales techniques

Not all sales techniques lend themselves to creating aligned need, value and profit.

As salespeople, we are not always blessed with the best of reputations either. In some quarters, selling still has a bad name, no doubt thanks to dubious sales practices that hopefully have been erased over the years. If you asked someone to consider words associated with a salesperson, you would typically hear things such as 'pushy', 'aggressive', 'hard-nosed', 'selfish' and 'liar'. I have asked this question many times and I have never once heard words such as 'kind', 'patient', 'good listener', 'ethical' or 'customer-centred'. Considering that this is the profession I am involved with, I find that somewhat embarrassing.

While some say that the birth of modern-day sales techniques was in the 1920–30 period, a swathe of sales training ideas and theories appeared from 1940 to the mid-1980s.

My first job in selling was in 1974, selling encyclopaedias door to door. I had never been on a training course before and I remember that the concept of objections was never bought up once on the course. The belief was that if we did not actually know about objections, we would never fear them or look out for them so then they would not be a problem – right? Well, in a superficial way, yes.

Because we toured different areas trying to sell these encyclopaedias each day and we knew we wouldn't be going back to that particular area, our job was to get people to sign up to a set on the night – no matter what it took. There was no 'cooling-off period' then, so if we got people to part with £50 to sign up, it was a done deal. That £50 was a lot of money back then – it equates to about £480 in 2020. Although my selling style has changed vastly since that day, pressure selling unfortunately still exists and is being practised by some less professional and probably less ethical salespeople.

If you want to read about the evolution of sales methods, visit www.bemoreeffective.com/theprofitsecret and if you are a first-time visitor, register and download the *Sales Evolution History*.

The need to change

We know selling has been around almost since the beginning of time and will no doubt be around for a long time to come, but:

- are we as salespeople learning lessons as the world changes?
- are we becoming more responsive and adapting to those changes?

Knowing that millions of salespeople have travelled down the same roads we travel today and had the same experiences, are we trying to reinvent the wheel, or can we react and adapt at the same pace of change that the world experiences today?

Jack Welch once said, "When change is happening outside your company faster that it is happening on the inside – the end is nigh." If that is true, then if change is happening outside the sales profession more quickly than it is happening inside our profession, where does that leave us?

And the one thing we all know about change is that it is constant; that is why we need to continually adapt our approach to selling to be effective.

Winning more sales at a higher margin may seem a lofty goal when it is arguably tougher today than it has ever been to win business profitably or produce sustainable growth. Businesses that have traditionally worked in partnership with certain suppliers face stiff competition from newly established businesses that are savvier or use a disruptive approach. The rapid spread of new markets, new opportunities and new players in any market, including yours, inevitably puts pressure on margins.

To make the situation even tougher, companies are doing business with fewer suppliers. Customers have unprecedented choice in terms of when, where and from whom to purchase, and by what means. Buyers are taking advantage of their strengthened negotiating position.

This point was reiterated to me at a sales conference. One of my co-presenters put a slide on the screen that read:

> What is the most dangerous word associated with professional selling today?

He asked the audience to think about what they thought was the answer to this question. What would you say is an answer to that question? Think about it for a moment.

People were saying things such as 'price' and 'discount'. I must admit that I was thinking along similar lines. Anyway, he then went on to reveal what he thought was the most dangerous word associated with professional selling: 'average'. Everyone went quiet for a moment. It wasn't the word people were expecting, I dare say. But the more I thought about that word 'average', the more I knew he was right. Because buyers are in a strong negotiating position today, so it is more and more likely that the 'average' salesperson is being hit with the price objection.

When average salespeople are confronted with price resistance, all too often they acquiesce, or show signs that they are tempted to give in; then it simply becomes a matter of 'how much' rather than 'if' or 'when'.

When faced with increased price resistance and the slower, more cautious buyer, the temptation for salespeople today is all too often to respond like an average salesperson. That means we give in on price. It means we are not smart enough to build a strong position of trust from which we can at least attempt to stand our ground, challenge their thinking or explain again the relevant and significant value on offer. It means we have forgotten that profit is sanity and sales merely vanity.

As salespeople, we know that our job is to defend the relevant value we have included in our proposal and to justify our price, but how often is that intention converted into action? What stops most salespeople translating known sales theory into practical solutions? It is that most salespeople think their job is to make sales rather than a profit.

That, my friends, is why profit is a secret. And the secret, I believe, to selling more at a higher margin.

CHAPTER 2

Building a sales proposition is like building a house

The Value House Sales Model

During 2010, I was delivering a series of sales training programmes for a large company based in central London. As this was an important client, I set up regular communication with each member of the sales team to help them implement the learning from the training sessions. I also encouraged them to contact me at any time with any situation or scenario that they would like to talk through or to get some help with.

Over the first few weeks, I noticed that the most common question I was being asked involved situations relating to price pressure. A typical request from one of the sales training delegates was along the lines of:

Salesperson: "I spoke to a prospect earlier today and he said he had received quotes from some of our competition and that our price was too high."

Me: "Have you already given the prospect a quote then?"

Salesperson: "Yes."

Me: "How did you get into a position to have put a quote in already?"

Salesperson:	"Well, he called in a few days ago and asked me about some products for a project he was working on, and he asked me to send him a quote if we could supply them."
Me:	"And what was your response?"
Salesperson:	"Well, I said we could supply them. I took a note of how much he needed and when, and sent him the quote the same day. I had great hopes for this enquiry, as he sounded quite keen."

I could sense immediately, as no doubt you can, that much was wrong here. My first thought was, 'Maybe if we had asked one or two further questions, as discussed in the sales training programme, we might not be in this position.'

Then I thought that if we had done things in a different order and had not been so reactive, that might have helped too. I wondered whether maybe that prospect wasn't the type of customer we really wanted to attract anyway. Each question in my head got me thinking we'd missed some fundamental principles during the conversation with the prospect and had, in fact, started the conversation in the wrong place to begin with.

I felt a bit like the Irish lad responding to a tourist who had asked for directions to Dublin, "Well sir, if I were you, wanting to get to Dublin, I wouldn't start from here."

If we wanted to win the sale, profitably, and help the other person discover something of relevant value, profitably, we would not start from here. It is not a great idea to start any sales conversation by simply sending a quote. Why? Because a quote is simply about product and price. And by starting the conversation about price, we are likely to find that the prospect continues to talk about the price; we are then far more likely to end up giving some, if not all, of our profit away.

Starting a sales conversation about price is about as sensible as placing the foundations of a house on sand. If you build a house on sand, it will move; the frame and walls will become unstable and the whole house, however valuable and handsome, will most likely collapse.

"But it is always about price!" I hear some of you shouting. No! It is never about price. It is always about the alignment of need, value and profit. Relevant value for them that is profitable for us. Profit is the forgotten key, the secret to selling more at a higher margin.

Building a sales operation or creating a proposal can be compared with building a house for sale. If you want to make a good profit from building and selling a house, you need to build it somewhere solid and sensible, put in appropriate foundations and create something that looks attractive and is filled with features the new owners will value. Getting it right in terms of location and build quality means that we will avoid most, if not all, heavyweight negotiations on the price.

The same is true for a business owner: if we get the foundations and build quality right in the sales operation of our company, or in a proposal, from the beginning, we can do a lot to avoid or minimise the amount of price resistance we get from our marketplace.

I am not a builder, so forgive my basic grasp of how to build a solid, strong, weatherproof and valuable house. May I suggest it consists of some essential steps, including:

- deciding where to build your house
- digging the foundations
- laying the cornerstones
- creating the framework of the house
- laying internal and external building blocks

- fitting a roof
- resolving the snags and dealing with any problems
- maintaining the house, to protect its value

I used the analogy of building a valuable house with my client and their sales team. With it, we challenged the use of quotations and in most cases changed them to 'business case proposals'. Surely that is just semantics?

No. A business case proposal had to include the prospect's declared need, its implications, the matching relevant benefits, the value our difference added and an estimated return on investment (ROI). Without those facts, the proposal could not be sent. Without engaging the prospect in a different type of conversation upfront, the business case could not be written.

From this was born a new sales approach to deliver relevant value for the prospects and clients as well as profit for the business: 'the value house sales model'. Here the key principles of building a house for sale are used as the analogy for building our sales operation and each sale, so that the perceived value is great enough to secure more sales at higher margins.

How can the value house sales model help sell more at a higher margin?

This approach is about how to modify our selling approach, as individual salespeople and as a company, so that we can sell more at higher margins by:

- creating the market perception that we are value-led rather than price-led
- systematising the selling of relevant value profitably
- avoiding or minimising the degree to which we get price resistance in our sales efforts

- responding in a positive and client-focused way to any price objections, to defend the relevant value and the profit

This method will reduce the amount and intensity of the average salesperson's nemesis: price pressure. Any good salesperson will tell you the best time to avoid an objection is before it comes up, so one mechanism of the Profit Secret is to adopt a preventive, not curative, approach.

When I think back to that presenter who suggested that the most dangerous word associated with professional selling was 'average', I see his point. 'Average' implies that most people are doing it, and with selling it is also true that there are too many people doing the same thing in an average way. Too many salespeople:

- are average planners
- set average goals, if any at all
- ask average questions – usually closed and predictable ones
- deliver average presentations that fail to offer relevant benefits to match declared needs
- take an average approach to closing; some avoid it altogether
- show an average response to price resistance; that is, they panic and crumble, giving up vital profit and making everyone's job harder

The Profit Secret promotes a mindset of excellence. Becoming excellent at selling, not sticking with average. Putting need, value and profit at the heart of every sale.

Throughout this book, you will discover many aspects to the Profit Secret: some about the sales environment of your business, some about proposals, closing sales, handling objections and, of course, the value house sales method.

The Profit Secret mindset and the value house sales method will help you increase the volume of sales you make at higher margins while minimising any price resistance along the way. They will help you write better sales proposals and run a more profitable sales operation.

> **I've created a guide to help you start putting these ideas into place, to download it visit www.bemoreeffective.com/ theprofitsecret and if you are a first-time visitor, register and download the *Value House Activity Worksheet*.**

Five ways the Profit Secret mindset enhances the sales process

1. Selling is a process: a process with defined steps that build on each other. As with physical exercise to build up muscle, every time you skip a step it reduces the possibility of a positive outcome. Selling is the act of proactively engaging a prospect in a series of steps, steps they consider relevant and meaningful, regardless of the outcome. Selling involves executing each step in a methodical way for every sales conversation – a repeatable framework for success. Taking shortcuts or eliminating steps only sets the salesperson up for failure.

2. The selling process must match the prospect's buying process. They are on a journey to buy something; that journey for them also has a series of steps. Each buyer may take a different path and is likely to move at a different pace. Imagine that both the buying process and the sales process are a dance. Ideally the salesperson needs to be dancing in harmony with the buyer, maybe a step ahead, leading in a synchronised way. Imagine the buyer doing a slow waltz and the salesperson doing the rumba. What is going to happen? Toes get squashed, legs clash and the dance ends badly.

3. Selling is a process of enabling discovery by the prospect. If the prospect doesn't discover something relevant and meaningful for themselves, then typically they don't have personal ownership of it. When a salesperson tells the prospect what they need rather than asking questions to facilitate the prospect's self-discovery, the probability of a buying decision is greatly diminished. After all, whose ideas do we like the most? Our own! And that is true for pretty much all of us, all the time. Parents quickly learn this with their children. If they can get their child to think that the idea of getting ready for school on time is their own idea and to their own advantage, the parent will have a better chance of getting out of the front door with less of a fight. Prospects are no different. They need to have ownership of the problems, needs, ideas, options and solutions being discussed in the sales process.

   Facilitating that discovery of a relevant and meaningful need by the prospect requires the salesperson to ask several probing questions. They reveal the prospect's situation, their problems or opportunities and the consequences of them. Most prospects didn't go to school to learn about selling or even about buying and decision-making, so it is highly unlikely they will be able to tell you their needs off the top of their head. In fact, most prospects will ask one of the last decision-making questions first, "How much will this cost me?" In most cases, you can help them by asking questions that cause them to think through a process to identify their needs. That's when real buy-in occurs.

4. Selling is the process of enabling someone to discover something of relevant value. The concept of need and its importance or relevance is driven and measured by the customer, not the seller, just as is the concept of value. People do not generally buy things they do not understand. People do not buy things that have no relevance to their needs or

desires. People do not buy features, however great, that do not provide a relevant and meaningful benefit. People do not exchange their hard-earned cash – whether business or personal – for things that do not appear to have a value, to them, greater than the cost.

Listen to your own questions of the prospect. Do they help them discover a relevant and meaningful problem or need? Do your questions help the prospect quantify the value of that need to themselves? Do your questions help the prospect to design the solution with you? Do your questions help them select the relevant and meaningful features and benefits? Do your questions enable the prospect to define the value in your offer or proposition for themselves? They must define the value for themselves and not have you define it for them. Your responsibility is to guide them along the path.

Listen to your comments, signposts, answers to questions and any presentations that you give. Do you know the difference between a feature statement and a value statement? Do you link every relevant feature back to an appropriate and meaningful need as well as a relevant and valuable benefit?

5. Selling is the process of enabling someone to discover something of relevant value to them, in a way that is profitable to us. Sales are vanity. Profit is sanity. Profit is the secret that makes sales and business operate authentically. The salesperson's job is to make profitable sales. That means an authentic and total acceptance of the fact that a sale is never won or lost on the price; that selling is always about the value: the value-cost equation of the need and the value-cost equation of the proposition. Selling is about increasing the perception of meaningful need and relevant value, in the prospect's mind, to the point that they no longer question or push back on the price.

CHAPTER 3

Where to build your business profitably

'Location. Location. Location'

Part of the secret to profitable sales and a profitable business is to know precisely where to look for great prospects and exactly who you are looking for. So, in this section, we are going to consider the elements that are important when deciding which marketplace is the best location for your business, including the make-up of an ideal prospect who will most easily become a profitable customer.

If we reflect on the housebuilding metaphor, this step is about choosing where you want your home to be. When building a house for sale, one of the key considerations is where to build it. You want to make sure the ground is strong, solid, level and stable and free from potential subsidence, so that your house stands firm, secure and safe. Even a well-built house with strong foundations can be swept away if built on shifting sands. If you choose to build your house on a steep, shaky and flaky hillside, the house will be impossible or expensive to build, and once built is highly unlikely to last.

The location itself must appeal to a certain type of company or person, the more of those certain types the better, because that gives you a greater chance of a sale. The volume of potential buyers, each highly attracted to the location, may also help you increase the price of your house because of the competition between them for something that appears to have been built for them. The more aligned the design of the house is to the dreams and requirements of those specific types of buyers the better, because it is more likely that you will be able to secure a higher price and therefore a greater profit.

Wouldn't the same be true if you wanted to build a profitable business? If you build your business on shaky ground, it is likely to collapse. What would shaky ground be? Building your sales operation in the wrong market, a limited market or an unstable or volatile market. Aiming your sales at the wrong type of customers or aiming to attract everyone, all types, or worse, no specific type at all. When you try to appeal to everyone, you attract no one.

Defining your target market

Part of the Profit Secret is to decide exactly who your audience is before you sell your services. Deciding on your target market is critical because that defined space, that defined group of companies with similar decision-makers, is the ground on which you lay the foundation for your business and for each sale. When you become clear about your target market, you will:

- know where to focus your research efforts. It is highly unlikely that you can know everything about everybody, while it is very possible for you to become an expert on a specific type of company and the most common type of decision-maker to be found there. To be an expert, you must understand your ideal customer, the organisation and the decision-makers, intimately. You need to be an expert in the problems they have, the way they do business and the language they speak. The greater your level of understanding, the more attractive you can make your business and proposition.

- know where to focus your selling and marketing efforts. Why run around everywhere, chasing all sorts of butterflies with a big net, when you can create a fragrant garden full of the favourite flowers and food of your single preferred type of butterfly?

Your target market is a specific group of companies and people to whom you will focus on selling highly relevant products and services. Whatever target market you choose, check to see that it meets the following criteria:

- Your target market has a big problem. They think about it all the time, it keeps them awake at night.

- Your target market wants their problem solved. The impact and cost of the problem is big enough that they will act to resolve it. Be warned: some people have problems with which they are quite happy to live.

- You can easily find your target market. If you want to catch sharks, you find out where sharks regularly eat and set up your baits and traps there. If you want to catch one type of butterfly, you work out what their favourite food is and set up your net next to that type of plant. Where do your prospects typically meet their peers, network or exhibit? What newspapers, magazines or blogs do they read? To what associations or institutes do they belong? With what social media outlets do they engage? While it may cost you time and money to find where people in your target market hang out, I promise you that it will be a worthwhile investment.

- Your target market has money to spend. There is no point having a terrific service if your target market does not have the money to pay for it. I know this sounds basic, but it's often overlooked. If the value you can deliver to your clients and the margin you can secure for yourself or your company are not high enough, what is the point?

- Your target market has a history of paying to have this problem solved. You want to focus on a target market with a proven track record of problems and people paying to solve them. A good sign is others selling products and services that aim to tackle a similar or related problem to the same target audience.

In addition, it is vital that you:

- have a passion for helping and serving this target market. Passion, which some would describe as enthusiasm, is an essential ingredient for selling your services. As the Chinese proverb says, "A man without a smiling face must never open a shop."

- have valuable expertise and experience you can offer. Your target market will want to buy from people who are experts in their field. Think about what specific expertise and experience you can offer your target market.

- have a different approach, product and service. While you don't always have to be better to win business, you do have to be different. If everything is the same, you are going to end up in a price war. In a price war, pretty much everyone loses, including the buyer. While you do not always have to be unique, you do need to have an uncommon advantage, something that sets you apart.

Targeting the right type of prospects

Part of the Profit Secret is to create value that others want to buy from you at a premium and thereby design out price resistance. Typically, we think of price resistance featuring during the final negotiation stages of a sale, when in fact it can be present throughout the buying process. Think about it – some people would not even go into certain shops, restaurants or hotels because they look too expensive, or too cheap. That is price resistance even before the prospect stage, let alone the closing stage.

It is important that we focus on the right type of prospects right from the start. One way to do this is to create a prospect targeting matrix.

This matrix will enable us to be objective about what type of organisation to focus our sales efforts on. It will also help us build value and profit, and avoid price resistance throughout the whole buying process. If we are not objective, we tend to decide who to focus our efforts on in a very subjective way, for instance:

"They're a big company, let's try them."

"They've got a great reputation; they must be worth calling."

Developing your prospect targeting matrix

So how do you prepare a target matrix for your company?

First, look back over 12 to 24 months at the customers you currently have. The organisations that buy a lot from you and like buying from you, despite the fact they could go elsewhere for a lower price. The ones you also enjoy working with, are profitable and do not tend to cause you much hassle. With customer relationship management (CRM) and sales ledger technology improving all the time, this information is probably readily available to you; if not, it is worth digging it out, however hard it is to find. Typically, these customers are the top-performing 20% in your sales ledger and may well be giving you 80% of your sales volumes and profits. That is based on the Pareto principle (also known as the 80–20 rule), which states that a small number of factors (20%) are responsible for the bulk of the results (80%). You may also find that 4% of your customers generate around 50% of your results.

Identifying common factors

Once you have worked out which organisations are already ideal customers for you, start looking for factors that most of those companies share. You probably need to consider a reasonable number of companies to do this – your top-performing 20% of companies may add up to between 20 and 50 organisations or more. You want common factors that are easy to identify, for example:

- Market sector (retail, engineering or local government, for example)

- Location (they all seem to be based in a certain area)
- Turnover or size (they all seem to fall within the same range)
- Business operating model (single site, multi-site, hub and spoke)
- Employee demographics (age, education level and income level)

What you consider to be an important factor will depend on what your business sells. For example, when I worked for American Express some years ago, one of the crucial elements of our targeting matrix was the number of employees a company had. This had a huge impact on the number of credit cards that could potentially be sold. With my medical employment agency, the hospital's focus on cardiac surgery was one of the most important factors, because the skilled doctors and nurses were highly paid and hard to find. For the employee engagement side of Be More Effective, the key factor is a combination of 1,000 or more employees and a multi-site operation, because those types of organisation generally have more internal communication problems.

It is likely that many of common factors you have identified in your customer base will apply to your ideal prospect. Write the factors down on the left-hand side of a piece of paper to begin developing your own prospect targeting matrix. Those factors listed in the table overleaf are only an example.

Target descriptions

Moving across three columns left to right, label them 'Ideal', 'Acceptable' and 'Unacceptable'.

Start with the 'ideal' column. Using your existing customers as a guide, write an ideal description for each factor listed. See the table here for examples.

Points	Ideal	Acceptable	Unacceptable
Turnover	£20,000,000	£5,000,000	£1,000,000
Location	South-West England	Southern England	North of Manchester
Industry	Construction Main Contractor	Construction Subcontractor	Non-Construction
Contact	Director	Operations Manager	Executive Assistant
Financial Picture	Healthy balance sheet	Two years of profit	Credit risk
Growth Pattern	Fast over five years	Single digit growth	In decline

Be as specific as you can. Go down all the factors writing the ideal as you go.

Then in the 'acceptable' column, write down characteristics that you deem acceptable for each factor. While not ideal, you would be reasonably happy to find a prospect that matched that description.

Once that is done, follow the same process in the 'unacceptable' column. Identify what you see as being unacceptable for each of the factors. If you came across a prospect that fitted the unacceptable description in one or more factors, you would turn them down, walk away – adios amigo!

Now you have a matrix that you can use to evaluate every prospect. You can measure what you know about them against each of the factors and determine the extent to which they are an ideal prospect for you to target.

What has this got to do with the Profit Secret? The more prospects you can identify that are close to the 'ideal' descriptions, the more likely you are to find new profitable customers, just like your current profitable customers. These high-performing customers like something about you and your products or services. They know something about your business that you may not – they, your market, are telling you something. "You are good for us; the value you give us is greater than the price we pay, and we like doing business with you."

With this group, you are likely to encounter less price resistance. Let's not fool ourselves here; this is no guarantee – it is all about minimising risk and exposure by design. The closer to the 'ideal' they are, the less likely it is that price resistance will appear with any frequency or severity. So, ask yourself a critical question before you go any further, "Can I grow my business by selling profitably to organisations like those highlighted in my prospect target matrix?"

If the answer is a big "Yes," let's look at the next set of key tools to use as we build our sales value house model. Remember that the aim is to improve the need, value and profit opportunity and to minimise, or design out, any price resistance.

Ideal prospect avatar

Once you have found your target market, the next step is to decide on the exact personality profile of your ideal client. The clearer you are about who you want to do business with, and why they will be specifically attracted to you, the more easily you will attract the clientele you're looking for. And their journey from prospect to client will be easier and quicker for you.

You are seeking to identify a specific individual with certain needs, concerns and desires who can be motivated to buy in the desired volumes at the optimal profit.

Consider their job titles, their key responsibilities, what is on their mind, their goals, worries and problems. Think about what and who influences them, their boss and their peers, their personal memberships, associations, charities and preferred brands. What do they read, watch and listen to? Consider who else in the marketplace is reaching out to them, how and what your prospect is likely to see and hear from these sources and channels. Think about what they talk about, how they present themselves to others, what behaviours and attitudes they demonstrate. Which communication channels are they most comfortable with? Phone, email, LinkedIn, Twitter, seminars or networking events?

A common tool for this approach is a prospect or customer avatar. How do I create this?

Brainstorm all the answers to the above prompts and questions. Use the people you already know as buyers in your top-performing customer organisations as a guide.

Once you have a long list, cluster common ideas together and begin to squeeze the words in a conceptual winepress to extract the key essence.

Here is an example:

CUSTOMER AVATAR

NAME: Nick
AGE: 40
GENDER: Male
MARITAL STATUS: Married
DEPENDANTS: 1 (age 19)
LOCATION: Hertfordshire

QUOTE: "Always looks on the bright side of life"
OCCUPATION: Sales Trainer
JOB TITLE: CEO
INCOME: £100,000
OTHER: Likes to run

GOALS AND VALUES

Goals:
- Increase training business
- Increase the capacity of his team
- Scale his business

Values:-
- Professional development
- Providing value for his clients
- Using value house sales model

CHALLENGES AND PAIN POINTS

Challenges:
- Scaling his training business
- Finding and retaining top trainers
- Leading edge sales skills

Pain points:
- Fear of losing business to people's indicision
- Keeping up with move to online delivery and digital content

SOURCES OF INFORMATION

Books:
Good to Great / Think and Grow Rich

Magazines:
Wired / Fast company

Blogs/Websites:
Scale his business

Conferences:
Thoughts on Thursday

Gurus:
Richard Denny / Tom Hopkins

Other:
All Monty Python material

OBJECTIONS AND ROLE IN THE PURCHASE PROCESS

Objections in the sale:
- Does the training fit an exisiting or new service he can monitise
- How long he and his team members will be 'out of pocket'

Role in the purchase process:
- Nick is the decision-maker
- Buys training to keep his team on top of the move to online delivery
- Motivated by value, not price
- Needs to believe the training can give his team and business the edge with online delivery

Ideal prospect statement

Next, work on a 15-word statement that has two parts.

The first part describes, in a few words, your ideal prospect and customer. The second part describes exactly how they use your products and services.

Here are two examples from clients:

1. A UK-based decision-maker who must protect his reputation, people, products and profits at any cost.

2. An influential leader demanding high standards and appreciating innovative, well-coordinated solutions delivered through trusted relationships.

While you won't feel the pain, sweat and tears others went through to create the words in those two examples, they will help you see the structure of the ideal prospect statement and give you something to aim at. You must put your own time, thought and energy into the process. As with anything, the more you put into the process, the more you gain. You are aiming for a set of words you can totally own, believe in and get seriously passionate about.

You now have three great market defining tools:

1. The prospect targeting matrix

2. The ideal prospect avatar

3. The ideal prospect statement

You also have a very clear understanding of where to build your value house sales model. You have the precise marketplace location of where to build profitable sales and a profitable business.

If you want the special guide that I've created to help you put these ideas into place, visit www.bemoreeffective.com/theprofitsecret and if you are a first-time visitor, register and download the *Prospect Targeting Worksheet.*

CHAPTER 4

Digging the foundations of profit and value

Proper prior planning prevents persistent price pressure

For a successful and profitable sales operation and for a salesperson who sells more than most and at a higher margin than most, there are several key elements to their approach. If you intended to build a house that you could sell easily and at a large profit, you would be advised, once the location was agreed, to create a plan. It is hard to imagine any housebuilder laying bricks randomly. A house built without a good plan and sound foundations will not be attractive, stable or worth much.

So, let us consider what these elements are.

It is vital that our business has a sales plan; as a minimum that should include a clear goal, a robust assessment of the current situation and a workable method of getting from A to B.

Remember that moment in Lewis Carroll's *Alice in Wonderland* when Alice arrives at a crossroads and the Cheshire Cat asks, "Where do you want to go?" Alice replies, "Why, I don't know." "Then any road will do," says the Cheshire Cat. You must first have a goal.

Imagine for a moment you were lost out in the wilderness, like Alice, trying to reach your goal. Before you took one step you would want to be sure that any step would take you in the right direction. That means you need to know something about your goal and your current location.

If you had a compass and you knew your destination was north of your current location, you could pinpoint north immediately. Once you know the direction to head in, you can be sure that any step you take is taking you in the general direction towards your goal.

Well, writing a plan serves the same purpose.

Planning brings the future into the present

We can use a series of thought processes to create plenty of exciting details for the three main parts of our plan:

1. What the future end state will be like, in as much detail as possible.

2. A reality check on where you are now in relation to the goal. With these two fixed points, the end and the beginning, you have a gap, so you can guess what the third aspect is, can't you?

3. The series of actions required to close that gap. A series of steps in the journey from our current situation to our future state. Every step in that journey from the current situation must link well with the next until our desired end is reached.

Planning is about bringing the future desired results into the present so we can do something to move us towards those goals today.

Strategic sales plan elements

1. **Objectives**

   Your important three-year sales goal supported by up to three key sub-goals.

2. **Current state profile**

   A robust assessment of the current state.

3. **Market analysis**

   Look at Chapter 3 for more on market dynamics and analysis.

4. **Customer and prospect focus**

   Look at Chapter 3 for more on prospect targeting.

5. **Growth strategies**

   A robust ease/benefit assessment of the different strategies.

6. **Lead generation strategies**

   Creating multiple channels of warm inbound leads using a variety of methods.

7. **Sales territory and pipeline plan**

   A sales territory plan for an individual salesperson or a sales team and a visual representation of prospects in the buying process.

8. **Sales strategies**

   A mixture of new business acquisition strategies and customer development strategies.

9. **Build your team**

   Businesses are built by teams. Even a solo sales entrepreneur needs support from suppliers, a bank and a good accountant. Who is in your team?

10. **Tools and systems**

    A CRM system, a customer and prospect-focusing tool and possibly strategic account development tools.

11. Metrics

The critical activity (lead) and results (lag) measures you are going to monitor and feed back to everyone involved.

12. Budgeting, Reports, Meetings and Sprint Plans

What will it cost to achieve your goal? What reports do you require? What type of meetings would aid alignment and accountability? What activity plans do we need?

1. Objectives

Think big, start small, grow fast. Goals work best when they are big enough to scare those involved a little. When achieving an objective means that you must do things differently rather than do the same things faster, it is likely to create a step change, which adds value to the goal. Goals take us to new levels. Zig Ziglar taught me plenty about setting goals and objectives; *See You at the Top* was for many years my favourite personal development book, surpassed only by *The 7 Habits of Highly Effective People* (Stephen Covey). Both will expand most people's view on goal-setting methods and benefits.

Dr Edwin Locke and Dr Gary Latham spent years researching the theory of goal-setting. They identified five elements needed for us to achieve our goals: clarity, challenge, commitment, feedback and task complexity. In his 1968 article, 'Toward a theory of task motivation and incentives', Locke showed how clear goals and appropriate feedback motivate employees. He highlighted that working on goals is a major source of motivation, which, in turn, improves performance. Locke showed that the more difficult and specific a goal is, the harder people tend to work to achieve it. So, think big!

Think as big as you dare; when you get near that peak, you will find another mountain to climb, for sure. If that is 25% more than you've ever achieved, then go with that – 50% or 100%? You decide. If you could not fail, what could you achieve in the next three years?

I am a big fan of Kaplan and Norton's balanced scorecard which looks at organisational performance from four perspectives. While this was designed as a business improvement tool, you can use the four perspectives to help you develop three supportive goals to your main sales goal. Those four perspectives are financial, customer, internal process improvement and innovation/learning. By setting goals in all four of those areas, you will move forward in a more sustainable way than by purely setting a single sales figure target of £x million.

Whatever goals and objectives you set must be clear. To ensure clarity, make sure each goal statement or objective is SMART; my version of this acronym used to test the precision of our goals is:

- **S**pecific
- **M**easurable
- **A**greed with all involved
- **R**elevant to all your other goals
- **T**imed by start and finish dates, while knowing the effort time required

2. Current state profile

The truth will set us free. We must be brave and review where we are as a business, sales operation and salesperson. We must be thorough enough in our review to find hard evidence to back up any opinions. There are many great tools and questions for creating a clear current assessment of your sales situation; here are some that will produce the most valuable insights.

Numbers first. Hard facts on the most important measures of activity and results. Sales results may be represented as revenue, gross profit, number of accounts opened, units sold, onboarding calls conducted or any specific measure that is relevant for your team or business. Most of these numbers can be run for a whole team, a region and for each salesperson. It is worth collecting and studying group averages and person-specific numbers.

Sales growth. Month-by-month and rolling quarterly or annual trends. Comparing the actual to target and previous years helps give a healthy perspective on how much progress you are or are not making. Growth is a fundamental mindset for you and every person in your team to have. A small blip in your trend line will do more than raise eyebrows: it will have your team digging into the details to find answers.

Lead growth. We are hardly going to grow sales if we don't have an increase in the number of leads coming to our business. Sustainable growth comes from having at least seven channels of marketing. Seven methods by which we send out attractive messages into the world of our ideal prospect. Each of these seven marketing channels needs to be producing inbound warm leads each month. The leads must be at the level and the quality to sustain the growth in sales that you require. If not, change the channels, the messages or both.

Lead conversion rate. The insights from conversion analytics help keep all of us in sales and marketing teams honest. It is a reality check on what type of prospect we are attracting through marketing channels with the messages we send out as well as how the prospect is reacting to the journey we take them on to become a customer. For some, lead-to-close conversion time provides useful insights.

Sales activity. Success comes from doing the right things, well enough and often enough. We must know what those right things or activities are. Telephone calls, decision-maker conversations, video calls, emails, face-to-face appointments, demonstrations, presentations, proposals, test runs or trials; each sales operation will have a slightly different sequence or emphasis on the steps that make up the journey a prospect takes to become a customer. Determine yours and be relentless at measuring them.

Activity conversion ratios. Activity conversion ratios give insights into whether we are doing something 'well enough'. In one of my businesses, I measured the rate at which phone calls converted into appointments and appointments converted into sales. I knew, at the end of year one, that we would hit our future sales targets provided each telesales person picked up the phone 80 times each day. Unless the skill levels of the whole team dropped, that single act was highly predictive of the results we would achieve. Finding a small number of highly predictive lead measures is very useful. We will talk about this more in the next chapter.

Proposal-to-close ratio. While this is included in the sales activity conversion above, it is important to highlight something now, which we will also cover in more depth later. Sending out a 'quote' to a prospect may often be the wrong thing to do. Prices and quotations can cause us more sales problems than we realise. Nevertheless, it is important to know the rate at which salespeople convert proposals into orders. This metric gives insights into the quality of leads, the quality of our sales processes and of course the skill of each salesperson.

Product or proposition review. Your efforts in attempting to sell at a higher price will yield better results if you have a good product that serves to meet your market needs. We discussed in an earlier chapter the need to establish what is most important to prospects. Making sure you have a product or service that satisfies those needs is critical. Even more critical is that you must also satisfy them in a way that your competitors do not.

- How does value, quality or service manifest itself in your offering to strike a meaningful difference?

- How are you different, better, quicker or faster than your competitors in areas that your prospects and customers find most important?

- In which aspects are you the same?

- In which aspects are you worse?

- It is well worth while investing time to conduct a SWOT (strengths, weaknesses, opportunities, threats) or SWT (strengths, weaknesses, trends in the market) analysis on your company, and also to conduct a SWOT on your top three competitors. Do the competitor SWOT analysis as if you worked for that company, and once you have written a fair and evidence-based SWOT analysis, work out five ways to beat each.

Product or service life cycle. Where you are selling multiple products or have multiple service offerings, it is important to track sales for each. There are two tools that will provide you with great insights into the current state and future potential of each offering you have: the product life cycle and the Boston matrix.

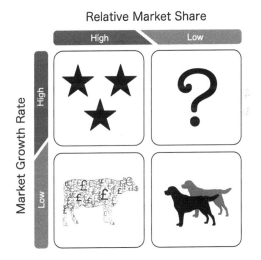

Where are each of your products or service offerings? It is important to know because the best methods for creating growth in sales and profits are different at each stage. And of course, while we can extend the life of some products in decline, it is vital to have enough new products starting their journey to fuel the growth we desire. Remember that while a new product may be exciting to sell, as an innovation often is, it can sometimes adversely impact sales of an existing star or cash cow product.

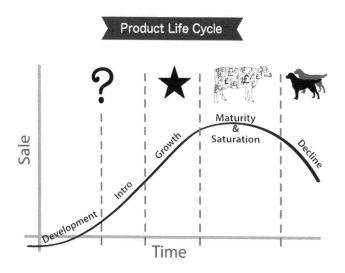

Average purchase value or average order value. This is one of the most useful measures of customer or client results because an effective way to increase sales revenue is to increase the average purchase value of each sale. Incorporating this measure into your analysis and tracking your historical trends is a smart strategy. For some businesses, it is also useful to measure the average length of projects and assignments.

Retention and churn rates, attrition rates and new or expansion monthly recurring revenue (MRR). These are particularly useful in subscription business models. Here we want to understand how many new customers join and how many previous subscribers leave each month. For a company to grow, it needs to add more new customers each month than the number who leave, while improving retention.

Customer lifetime value (CLV) is a measure of the net profit a company makes from any given customer group. CLV is an estimate of a typical customer's monetary worth to a business after factoring in the value of the relationship over time. While you would normally recalculate this once or twice a year, it is certainly a worthwhile exercise in a robust current state review. To calculate CLV, you need to calculate average purchase value, and then multiply that number by the average purchase frequency rate to determine customer value. Then, once you calculate average customer lifespan from your attrition rates, you can multiply that by customer value to determine CLV. This measure generally uses a net profit figure, or net profit contribution figure; if it is hard to get at that data, then even a figure based on the average gross profit is worth knowing.

Customer Lifetime Value
is the net profit contribution to the company over time

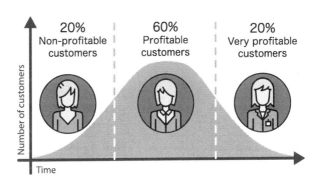

You should also establish the cost of sale and track this regularly as part of measuring CLV. Both are useful to have when thinking about what it is going to cost you to grow by x number of customers each year, because you will also know how much gross profit or net profit each will generate over the average customer lifetime.

Net Promoter Score® (NPS®) measures customer experience and predicts business growth. Developed by Bain & Company,

Inc, with Satmetrix Systems, Inc and Fred Reichheld, this proven measure has transformed many businesses around the world and now provides the core measurement for most customer experience management programmes. You calculate your NPS by asking all your customers to answer a key question, using a 0–10 scale:

> How likely is it that you would recommend [brand] to a friend or colleague?

The replies are then grouped as follows:

- **Promoters** (score 9–10) are loyal enthusiasts who will keep buying and refer others, fuelling growth.

- **Passives** (score 7–8) are satisfied but unenthusiastic customers who will buy from anyone.

- **Detractors** (score 0–6) are unhappy customers who can damage your brand and impede growth through negative word-of-mouth ratings.

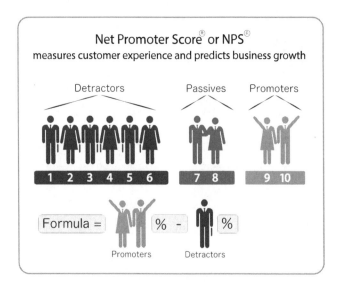

Some businesses measure this constantly, offering the opportunity to provide feedback after every transaction. Some survey the client base monthly, quarterly or annually. An NPS of 70% is world-class; most companies score between 0% and 22%. Knowing your current score is a vital part of the current state and highly predictive of future growth. Even a single salesperson in a larger team would be advised to ask their own customers for an NPS, if the business was not using NPS.

Customer journey review. As part of creating the current state assessment, it would make sense to review the customer journey, as well as key internal processes, asking questions such as:

- What is working?
- What is not working?
- What are your frustrations?
- What is missing?

Salesperson audit. What are your top salesperson's competencies? What are their habits, skills and attitudes, and what knowledge do they have? How well do they match the ideal competency model? In what ways does the sales compensation model drive the right behaviours, the right quality and the right frequency? In what ways does it not? What would happen if you simply added more people to the sales team? Would that yield a greater result? If not, why? If so, what is stopping you from doing that?

3. Market analysis

You will remember this from Chapter 3.

4. Customer and prospect focus

This was also covered in Chapter 3.

5. Growth strategies

Conducting a robust assessment of the different paths to growth you are using is a vital part of the Profit Secret. Having a scalable and profitable business and sales pipeline begins in the design. One model to challenge your thinking is the Ansoff matrix.

Developed by Igor Ansoff in 1965, this is one of the most used tools for this type of analysis, thanks to its simplicity and ease of use. The output from the Ansoff matrix analysis is a series of potential growth strategies. Which of the four quadrants is the easiest, quickest, most sustainable, most profitable route to growth?

Market penetration means focusing on selling existing products into existing markets. You seek to increase the market share of current products in your current market. This means finding ways to persuade your current customers to order more frequently or increase their average order value of current products, or ideally both, while also improving customer retention rates.

It may require finding ways to drive out competitors, dominate your current market and acquire new customers from the same target market with similar types of problems and needs. If you increase the number of customers while holding on to the ones you already had, you grow as a direct result. The market penetration strategies are generally lower cost, faster and easier to implement.

Heinz used a market penetration strategy to fight back after losing market share during 2012 and 2013. In 2014, it fought back with the 'It has to be Heinz' advertising campaign in Europe. It made no statements about the products' features, benefits or price. Instead the ads showed parents putting ketchup on their children's meals and suggested that some things just weren't the same without Heinz. The nostalgic campaign successfully pushed their market share back up.

Product development involves introducing new products into your current market and to current customers. The new product or service may be a derivative of your current offering, which may help you differentiate yourself from your competition. It may help you leverage a new trend in your marketplace. A marketplace is not static; if you are not adding new offerings into the mix each year, you are being left behind. The derivatives of what you do now will probably make you more money in the long term than you do now.

The Coca-Cola Company used product development. While Diet Coke was a success, it was attracting females more than males, overwhelmingly so. Men don't drink it because they think of it as a 'softer' drink for the ladies. What did Coca-Cola do? It didn't try to re-educate the hard men about the errors of their ways; it gave them Coke Zero, which offers the same benefits as Diet Coke and was designed from a marketing and sales proposition point of view to be a 'guy's drink'. This product development idea opened a whole new niche.

Market development means seeking to sell your existing products into new markets. There are many possible ways of using this type of strategy, including selling your products into a new country and trying new distribution channels, such as selling via an e-commerce website, or through resellers or agents. Some questions to answer if you want to consider this:

- How can we extend our current market into a different 'space?'

- What are some new market sectors where prospects would have similar and relevant needs?

- What are some geographical areas, territories or countries where prospect would have similar and relevant needs?

Market development strategies often cost more than market penetration strategies and may take longer to produce results.

Diversification involves selling new products in new markets. This is generally seen as a more risky, costly or at least longer term strategy. This is because you are trying to enter an unfamiliar market, where you have no current customers, therefore little or no experience. You are trying to sell a product that is unfamiliar to you. If the product is new just to you, there may be plenty of evidence of the benefits and ROI for the prospects to mull over. If it is a new product to them too, you have the challenging job of finding the early adopters who are the ones willing to try something new.

If you are going to adopt a diversification strategy as your main path to growth, you should have a clear idea about what you expect to gain from the strategy, along with a robust and evidenced-based assessment of the risks. When you get this balance between risk and reward right, a marketing strategy of diversification can be highly rewarding – being first to market with a new, popular product can be highly profitable.

While the Ansoff matrix is a great tool, it should not be the only tool you use to select your final growth strategy. You need to consider the market dynamics and the ideal prospect, as we did earlier, for your current market as well as other external factors.

If you want the special guide that I've created to help you start putting these ideas into place, visit www.bemoreeffective.com/theprofitsecret and if you are a first-time visitor, register and download the *Strategic Sales Plan Worksheet*.

CHAPTER 5

Laying the cornerstones of profit

Lead generation strategies – your first cornerstone

This is No. 6 from the strategic sales plan elements. Now before you say, "I am a salesperson," and that 'marketing' is someone else's job, remember that marketing makes sales possible. If you want to sell more, more easily and at a higher margin, creating a bigger pool of warm leads to convert will pay you admirably. Each salesperson is, in one sense, a solo entrepreneur, a business professional. You've probably heard this before: give a man a fish and feed him for a day; teach him to fish and feed him for a lifetime. Learning to generate your own leads, in addition to those that come through anyone else, will pay you handsomely.

Sustainable growth comes from having at least seven different channels that produce warm inbound leads each month. These warm leads are generated because you send out attractive marketing messages through those channels, frequently. You choose those specific channels because they give you access to a large pool of your ideal prospects and customers. Those messages are attractive to your specific ideal prospect and customer, so naturally some respond.

In marketing and in sales you can either create a big butterfly net and run around madly chasing butterflies and moths, hoping to catch the ideal one, or you can create a fragrant garden attractive to the specific butterfly you want to catch and have them find you.

How do I know this? I wasted hours trying to catch a day-flying hawkmoth with a friend, wandering from field to field across part of the Loire Valley in France. My buddy was an expert on these moths, and I was tagging along for the fresh air. We caught zero, none, nothing. Right at the end of the afternoon we came across a red valerian bush that had about six of these moths hovering over it. "Why are all these moths gathered at this particular bush?" I asked my buddy. "Because," he said, "that flower is one of their favourite food sources." From then on, I merely looked for red valerian plants and surprise, surprise, we found all the moths he needed.

Your channels could include events, trade shows, exhibitions, newspaper or magazine advertising or editorials, public relations, television or radio ads, direct mail, email, your website, paid search, search engine optimisation (SEO) and conversion rate optimisation (CRO), social media outlets, including LinkedIn, endorsements, a book, a blog, a video channel, networking and third-party referral systems.

> Stop reading now and download the brilliant *Lead Generation Audit Worksheet* I've created at www.bemoreeffective.com/theprofitsecret and if you are a first-time visitor, register and download the worksheet.

How did you do? What do you mean you haven't completed the worksheet yet? Are you crazy? That worksheet will give you lots of ideas to improve your lead generation and your sales.

Six key lead generation strategies anyone can use

Here are six very productive lead generation strategies that any business or individual can use. You can interweave these six strategies with your seven chosen channels. Developed by Robert Middleton, founder of Action Plan Marketing, as part of his approach, they have served many businesses large and small very well. Originally written for a typical consulting business, but widely adopted by other types of business, the six main strategies are:

1. **A writing strategy.** How could you gain more credibility by communicating your expertise and value? A book? A blog? An article for an industry magazine?

2. **A speaking strategy.** How could you stand out as an expert, as someone who adds value everywhere you go? A webinar or through chambers of commerce? Industry associations?

3. **A keep-in-touch strategy.** How are you going to stay in regular contact with your prospects, your customers and others in your network who can refer you on? However you do this, it must be relevant, credible and add value.

4. **A referral strategy.** How can you encourage those who know you and trust you already to refer you on? How can you refer those in your network to each other? Remember – givers gain. If you want referrals, give some.

5. **A networking strategy.** How can you gain visibility and credibility in a relevant network of peers? If you wanted to catch sharks, you would fish where they gather to eat. Where do your ideal prospects and customers gather to network? How could you add value to be a part of those meetings?

6. **A direct outreach strategy.** Even warm qualified leads must be followed up. How are you going to do that? And do remember, while warm leads are far more easily converted, having a direct outreach strategy to cold relevant prospects does still work.

Sales territory and pipeline plan – your second cornerstone

This is No. 7 from the strategic sales plan elements. A sales territory is generally seen as a specific prospect and customer group or a geographical area for which an individual salesperson – maybe you – or a sales team is responsible. Territories can also be divided by potential, industry, product, customer type, purchase history and referral source.

Studies show that effective territory management can increase overall sales, improve customer coverage and reduce costs. That is another part of the Profit Secret, even if it involves simply planning your own patch as a solo salesperson or business owner.

Your challenge is to consider the optimum territory structure to accomplish your sales and profit targets by blending the resource and people you have with the requirements your market and your goals place upon you; balancing the workload to acquire new customers while developing your existing customers as efficiently as possible. It is essential to have the right amount of time and resource to ensure coverage of your target market without over-resourcing, even if that is to maximise face-to-face time with prospects and clients and minimise driving time. Increasing time spent face-to-face will usually increase sales.

To help you prioritise, think about the following:

1. **Decide how far you can reach on a patch**

   You cannot be everywhere, even if you think you are omnipresent. Learning to prioritise is part of the Profit Secret. Your total available market (TAM) is the entire body of businesses and your serviceable available market (SAM) is all consumers on the territory. Targeting both would waste your time and money.

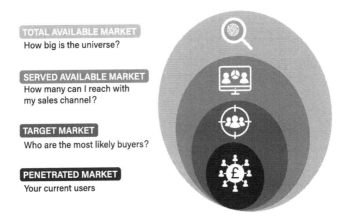

TOTAL AVAILABLE MARKET
How big is the universe?

SERVED AVAILABLE MARKET
How many can I reach with my sales channel?

TARGET MARKET
Who are the most likely buyers?

PENETRATED MARKET
Your current users

How can you produce warm leads purely from the target market and the penetrated market (customers)? Dominate the minds and desks of those in a niche rather than risk your message being spread so thin that no one notices.

2. Assess prospect and customer account quality in a territory

Who are the top clients, say the top 20%? They gave you 80% of your sales last year and will do so again if you look after them well enough. Who are the top 4%? They gave you close to 50% of your business last year. These you must develop. They are mission critical.

Who are the top prospects? Who could be another top 20% client? Another 4% client? The top 4% prospects are 'catapult prospects', so called because they can catapult your sales and profits to a new level. How can you maximise the use of time, effort, resources and money into the development of these two groups? The bulk of your growth will come from these.

Remember your current sales pipeline. Unless you are starting your sales operation from scratch, you will have a certain number of prospects at various stages in your pipeline. In your current state profile, you will have worked out average order values and lead conversion ratios and sales activity conversion ratios. So, if you know how many leads are in the pipeline and the value of them, you can forecast what is likely to come out the other end in sales pretty accurately.

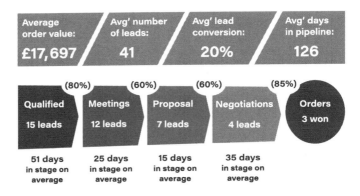

Pipeline Assessment Example

3. Assess the relative rank of all territories

Where you have multiple territories, it is important to rank them. Determining which sales territory supports which areas of the sales funnel and what volume of sales and profit will cause you to think about the time, effort, resource and people you bring into play. Score your territories as high, medium or low value, for example.

4. Where do you put your best reps?

If you have multiple territories and reps, now comes the crucial step of assigning the best rep to the patch where they are most likely to create the most growth. Which set of competencies, (knowledge, attitudes, skills and habits) is most applicable to maximise the development of each set of accounts? By strategically assigning the best qualified reps to the patch that most closely matches their competencies, you will empower them to succeed while ensuring that prospects and clients receive the most favourable attention and service.

5. Set goals and targets

Whether you're mapping out a new territory management plan for a sales team or redefining your approach to your own sales territory, remember to set clear SMART goals. The easier your goals are to measure and track, the better. You are going to need lead or activity goals as well as lag or result-based goals – whether you are a solo salesperson or leading a team of 600. Set everyone lead and lag targets. Remember that success comes from doing the right things, well enough and often enough. The farm that produces the results is activity. Activity is the constant. So, what should those activities be; how often and to what standard should they be undertaken in order to achieve the result? Build your sales activity targets by reverse engineering the pipeline with the current conversion ratios.

If you want to achieve sales worth £1m next year, start by calculating the number of deals you need to close to achieve that revenue. If your average deal size is £20,000, then you'll need to close 50 deals to achieve your goal. Fifty deals a year is slightly more than four deals a month and almost one a week, which sounds simple enough. You can easily translate that result into activity levels required by analysing your pipeline and the key conversation ratios. This we discuss in detail later in this chapter.

All things being equal, if last year's conversation ratios and average order values remain the same this year, you know what you and your team have to do, in terms of activities. Doing the right things well enough (CRO) and often enough (activity targets) leads to success (your sales target).

Provided the activity numbers feel doable, this breakdown of results into activities normally builds confidence in ourselves and our team. Confidence based on hard evidence – not blah-blah.

Speaking of blah-blah, even a well-thought-out set of activity numbers is typically blah-blah, if there are no names. It is vital to set client-related targets. If 50% of your sales are going to come from 4% of your clients and prospects, who are they? What are the sales results and the sales activity goals related to each of those catapults? If 20% of prospects and customers will give you 80% of your sales, can you name all these too?

6. Decide on your sales and marketing strategies

We've already mentioned a range of lead generation strategies; which ones are going to produce the number of warm inbound leads that you need? In the next section we will discuss sales strategies, so you can select your preferred options from that section.

7. Track your results, review and revise. Ready – Fire – Aim

This last step continues until you rewrite the whole plan, maybe in a year's time. It is vital to measure your progress and growth continually. What gets measured usually gets done and what gets analysed and fed back to the people involved usually improves. Ready – Fire – Aim. Write the plan, act on the plan, learn from life's rich tapestry, called feedback and adjust.

If any of your territories or reps are overperforming or underperforming, find out why and implement improvements. Share the love – well, at least the best practice. Remember to calculate the costs involved as well as the various activities and results. This book is called *The Profit Secret*, not *Vanity Fair*; sometimes costs creep up faster than sales results or profit margin, and sometimes people have started discounting to get something over the line. Which line counts? The bottom line: profit.

Sales strategies – your third cornerstone

This is No. 8 from the strategic sales plan elements. Your sales strategies are a mix of pragmatic new business acquisition approaches along with the existing customer business development tactics. These are the methods by which we can determine whether we're doing the right things, well enough and often enough.

Talking about being pragmatic, instead of describing these key ideas in nice waffling terms, how about some straightforward examples?

Four new business acquisition strategies and tactics

1. Think of seven activities to help you exceed your sales quota for new clients:

   - Send xx letters or emails of introduction to new warm leads each week.

   - Connect with xx warm leads or appropriate cold prospects on LinkedIn.

   - Make xx calls of introduction to new warm leads each week.

   - Make xx face-to-face contacts with new warm prospects each week.

   - Create xx proposals each week.

   - Your turn – think of two more.

2. Think of seven ways to increase awareness in the marketplace of your products, services, and solutions:

   - Join and participate in three professional associations to which your best prospects and customers belong.

- Purchase the mailing lists of these associations and send letters of introduction or contact with them on LinkedIn.

- Join and participate in three professional online forums to which your best prospects and customers belong; most importantly, participate in one of them for 15 minutes a day.

- Attend all trade shows and conventions that your best prospects and customers attend, find out who is going, arrange face-to-face meetings at, before or immediately after these events; work the floor when there.

- Take a stand at the best trade exhibition, invite everyone on your database, let the world know you are there, run competitions, quizzes or some kind of relevant fun experience; make your stand, stand out – even if it is only a small 2m table.

- Your turn – think of two more.

3. Seven ways to obtain referrals for new customers:

    - Within 30 days of delivering your product, service or solution, follow up each new customer to ensure that they are delighted. If they are not delighted, resolve this so that you can go back to seek customer referrals. If they are delighted, ask them for their 'help' in finding someone who may have some of the problems they used to have.

    - Ask everyone in your network the same question, "Can you help me?" Your wealth is in your knowledge and your network if you leverage both. The more people you ask, the more introductions you will receive. Make it a habit. Ask for one introduction every day.

    - Create an incentive for both parties: the person making the introduction for you and the new prospect. That could be a £5 gift voucher, or a discount off their next order.

- Host exclusive, invitation-only events (real or virtual) where you allow your invited guests to bring a friend or colleague.

- GIVE referrals. Givers gain. Join up the dots in your network; leverage your knowledge and your network to benefit someone else. It will come back to you 10 times over.

- Your turn – think of two more.

4. Seven ways to land a catapult client this year:

   My first catapult doubled the size of my business. It took me a year to win them over from the incumbent supplier. That contract was worth more than £237,000 gross profit each year after that.

   - List seven prospects who could each double the size of your business.

   - List seven prospects who could generate 10 times the average spend per year by your typical client.

   - Select three catapult prospects and research pain points relative to your product and service.

   - Find four contacts associated with each catapult prospect: a source of information; a person who owns the 'ideal problem' for you to solve; the person who holds the budget; and the ultimate source of power who can decide whether you are the right answer regardless of the price.

   - Decide how best to approach each. Who could introduce you? Do one thing each week to reach out to each of the catapult prospects. Once you get into serious conversations with one of them slow down your rate of approach to the others. It better to land one aircraft at a time on an aircraft carrier.

   - Your turn – you think of two more things.

If you want the full *New Business Acquisition Guide* that I've created to help you start putting these ideas into place, including growing faster with Pareto prospects and leveraging your network, visit www.bemoreeffective.com/theprofitsecret and if you are a first-time visitor, register and download the guide.

Existing customer development strategies and tactics

1. Create a touch-point programme:

    - Contact each of your existing top 20% customers once each month with a new idea they cannot get from anyone else.

    - Ensure that everybody in your business knows the top 4% of customers and their key contacts by name, to improve the quality and speed of response to any inbound contact.

    - Plan and schedule a programme of proactive phone calls, visits, net promoter review and account review meetings for each of the top 20% clients.

    - Plan and schedule an annual or biannual managing director to managing director meeting for each of the top 4% clients.

    - Organise a lunch meeting each month; invite three happy customers and one prospect. Make it clear who is paying – you, or each for their own?

    - Your turn – think of two more things.

2. Seven strategic account development strategies:

    - Introduce yourself to three other departments, divisions or teams within each of your larger existing customer accounts.

- Ask each of your existing customer contacts to introduce you to one other department in their organisation that is impacted by the types of pain points relevant to your products and services.

- Most good chairs have four or more legs. How many people recognise you by sight and name when you walk around their facility? Ensure there are four or more senior people who know you well.

- Work out the personality style of each contact using a model such as empathy styles or personality styles indicator (PSI) so you can tailor your approach to them.

- Personally meet a top executive at each of your top customers twice each year.

- Your turn – think of two more ways to develop your key accounts.

3. Seven cross-selling strategies:

   Selling more of what you already have, or know how to do, to people who already know, like and trust you is a fast and cheap route to grow your profits. One of my clients thought he had 12,000 customers who bought from a range of 45,000 stock-keeping units (SKUs). Analysis showed that there were sales of more than £1,000 for only 657 SKUs in that year; and only 256 customers spent more than £1,000 in the same period. We started a cross-selling campaign, to sell 657 products to all 256 customers while delisting 13,000 SKUs (nearly 30% of 45,000) and recovering dead cash tied up in stock gathering dust. Sell more of what you are known for, and best at, to the people who love you the most. Simples.

   - Create a truth chart. List your accounts on one axis of a table and all your products on the other. Work out which accounts buy which product or service – how much and how often. Then work out the potential for each product or service in each account. Prioritise the best opportunities and go and sell something.

- Create a case study and a video testimonial with your best contact in each of your top performing accounts. Show these to different clients to support your proposals for them to take something new from you.

- Pitch the 'power of three' as an upselling habit. This means giving the client three options for their cross-sale purchase: the need, the want, and the dream. Good. Better. Best.

- Aim to increase the number of items on any order. Make those add-ons relevant, while at a smaller cost to what had been ordered already. Adding £50 to a £500 order is easier than trying to add £500 to a £50 order.

- Your turn – think of three more cross-selling strategies.

4. Social media strategies to help develop customers relationships:

> 78.6% of salespeople using social media outsell their peers. (Forbes, May 2013)

In his article 'The Rise of Social Salespeople', Jim Keenan, a social sales specialist, argues that using social media to sell increases profits as well as improving sales conversion ratios. Social media is a powerful communication platform and communication will always be at the heart of selling. Social media enables you to engage with people, read what is important to them and post news and information that is relevant to them, creating a fragrant garden to attract your specific type of butterfly. Or to act by approaching them at just the right time.

Actively connect widely across your industry, on as many platforms as you can manage. Connect with your clients, prospects and peers – then read and listen to what they say. It is the closest thing to being a fly on the wall in your customers', prospects' and competitors' worlds. Social media gives you information that is almost impossible to obtain through traditional means. A lead today can be someone complaining on Twitter or Facebook that their current supplier is driving them crazy. It can be a question in a LinkedIn group. Develop the habit of investing 15 minutes a day engaging on social media, listening and responding.

> **For more ideas on speaking strategies and the multi-channel communication strategy ideas, visit www.bemoreeffective.com/ theprofitsecret and if you are a first-time visitor, register and download the *Existing Customer Development Strategy Guide*.**

Measure the results

Sales and marketing plans are always evolving because the world from which we are planning to secure sales is always evolving.

We need to know where we are, based on evidence, against our original plan. We need to know what's working and what isn't, or we will not know what and how to improve. Don't do what you can't measure, and don't measure what you can't or won't change. Choose measures you can act on.

The pipeline report by month is probably the best tool for effective sales management and accurate forecasting. It should show you visually the number and value of opportunities at each stage and of course those expected to close this month, next month and thereafter by quarter through to the end of the year.

A study by Jordan and Kelly (*Harvard Business Review*, January 2015) found that there was an 18% difference in revenue growth between companies that had a defined formal sales process and those that did not. Furthermore, companies that mastered three specific pipeline practices had 28% higher revenue growth. Now you'd think in a book entitled *The Profit Secret* that I might tell you what those three things are rather than leave you to guess, wouldn't you? Oh, all right then – those three things are:

- Clearly define the sales process consistently applied across the business.

- Invest at least three hours each month in reviewing and managing each salesperson's pipeline.

- Train the sales managers on pipeline management.

Sales pipeline

Imagine the whole sales process like a pipeline as illustrated here:

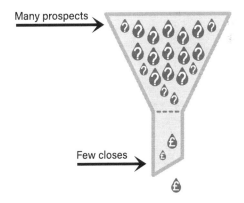

You can see at the very end of the process is where we want to be, with a sale. You'll also notice at the very beginning of the pipeline are people we choose to put in the pipeline. The output of our sales pipeline will only ever be as sizable as the input. We can work as diligently as we like, with a voracious work ethic, but if we are working on the wrong type of prospects then we will NEVER achieve the success we would like because most of the people taking our time have little interest in buying our products or services.

If we **'fish where our target prospect eats'**, we have a higher probability of achieving the type of success we would like to achieve. This means making sure that most of the prospects we put into our pipeline are the type who are likely to have the biggest need for and interest in our products.

Work out your key ratios

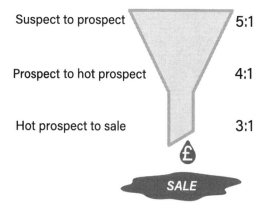

Suspect to prospect   5:1

Prospect to hot prospect   4:1

Hot prospect to sale   3:1

SALE

The key ratios are the conversion rates from one stage of the process to the next. For example, if you make 20 telephone calls to secure one appointment, then your ratio for that area of activity is 20:1. A lot of effort and time has gone into securing one appointment. In a generic sales pipeline, a salesperson could have ratios in the following ranges:

- Suspect to prospect (5:1)
- Prospect to 'hot' prospect (4:1)
- 'Hot' prospect to sale (3:1)

You may have different ones, depending on your experience, sales cycle, industry, competition and other factors, but let's use these for illustration purposes. When you do this activity for yourself later, you may find that your ratios are different.

Suspect to prospect (5:1)

This is the type of company you suspect could become a prospect. You need to do further research to find out if what you suspect is true and that they are indeed a prospect.

Prospect to 'hot' prospect (4:1)

The difference between a prospect and a 'hot' prospect is simply the degree of qualification achieved. They are not a sale yet, but you are pretty sure they are a serious contender.

'Hot' prospect to sale (3:1)

A sale arises when the prospect has given you a verbal and written go-ahead and it is a firm arrangement. We can see even now that despite careful attention to qualifying throughout our pipeline, some still do not make it. In this example, two prospects do not become a sale at this time. While the specific individuals might become a sale in the end, the average 12-month closing ratio is likely to remain the same, 3:1.

That two prospects fall at the last hurdle is disheartening. All that time and effort has been invested so far, only to find it come to nothing. It certainly is worthwhile looking back and learning some lessons so you can fail forwards. It is worth mentioning now that it is common for a hot prospect to decide to do nothing and not buy from anyone. Around 60% of the time, not deciding is likely to be the explanation for the 'no' outcome. A lack of a decision – rather than the incumbent supplier – is more often your true competition. That is part of the Profit Secret.

Here is another Profit Secret. Successfully selling at a conversion rate of 50% or more requires the prospect to discover the answers to the following questions with you:

- What is the evidence that the prospect should change at all? What is the cost of doing nothing?

- What evidence is there that the prospect should change now, rather than later?

- What is the evidence that your approach offers the least risk of all available options, including 'doing nothing'?

If you cannot get satisfactory answers to all three questions, you would be better off recognising that early, and changing your sales strategy or qualifying yourself out, rather than throwing even more time and effort at a lost cause.

Lost sale review

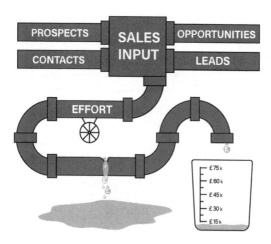

Knowing the reasons why a 'no' didn't become a sale by asking the prospect afterwards is an insightful process. Asking the prospect to list the reasons they went elsewhere or did nothing helps you narrow your own search for improvements.

- How could I have identified that earlier by asking better questions?

- What other questions could I have asked?

- How could I have pre-empted that concern earlier in the sales process?

- How could I have answered the concerns with a better explanation?

- Should I have chosen to put them in the pipeline to start with?

- How could the pipeline be tighter and more effectively targeted to attract prospects who are more likely to buy?

Asking these types of question is vital, because the pipeline and our ratios are our lifeblood. The pipeline is what we can influence. A salesperson's giddy heights of success or lows of mediocrity all have one thing in common – a pipeline. The quantity and quality of the activities associated with it determine our results.

If you could put in the same sales effort and get more customers, more sales, and achieve a higher profit, would you do it? Of course you would. Finding out about your pipeline, analysing your ratios, and thinking about things you could do to improve will help you achieve just that.

Sales velocity

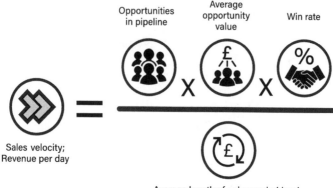

This is the measurement of how quickly prospects move through your pipeline and generate revenue. The sales velocity equation uses four measures: number of opportunities in the pipeline; multiplied by average expected order value; multiplied by your win rate; over the average length of days opportunities stay in the pipeline. This determines how much revenue you can expect your prospects to generate over a specific period.

Why does this equation matter? Think about it; if you increase all three factors on the top by 10% each and reduce the bottom measure by 10% your sales revenue increases by 47%. Go on, you do the calculation.

Objective qualification

In conjunction with that, it is worth considering having an objective system of forecasting other than the subjective method that average salespeople and sales managers typically use. Overleaf is an objective example you can build on.

Qualification levels

90%	You have
	• identified a clear need you both agree on
	• presented a solution which has been positively received by most of the committee as the ROI stacks up
	• a verbal decision to go ahead
	• not received written confirmation
	• been dealing with the decision maker
	The client
	• has evidence that they must do something now
	• agrees that cost and risk of doing nothing is greater than our solution
	• is not talking to anyone else
80%	You have
	• identified a need you both agree on
	• presented a solution that has been warmly received by most of the committee as the ROI stacks up
	• been dealing with the decision maker
	The client
	• has indicated that they must do something
	• has made no commitment yet
60%	You have
	• met the prospect more than once
	• met most people on the committee
	• identified a specific tangible need
	• identified an impending event for them
	• not yet presented your solution yet
30%	• The client has agreed to meet
	• Your research shows evidence that they may have a need for your product or service

Other factors to consider

1. How many people on the decision-making committee have you met? Ideally you need to meet the majority and win them over. You need at least four legs on your chair with most deals. Remember the legs from earlier?

- The source of power
- The owner of the problem
- The person with the money
- A source of information

2. Ideally you want an internal coach or white knight on the inside who sells for you when you are not there and guides you when they can.

3. How long and thorough has the sales process been?

4. Download the Be More Effective app from the App Store or Google Play and use the Sales Predictor function.

> **If you would like the extra guide to improving your sales pipeline and sales velocity, visit www.bemoreeffective.com/ theprofitsecret and if you are a first-time visitor, register and download the *Improving Sales Pipeline Guide*.**

Simplify, simplify, simplify

Do you want your sales and marketing people to use the plan on a daily, weekly and monthly basis? If so, it will need to be blisteringly simple, clear and highly actionable.

I am a great believer in one-page plans. Whether it is a one-year business plan or a one-year sales and marketing plan, we should be able to get the critical elements down to one page. Everyone in the team can have a copy of the team plan and develop a one-page plan of their own.

CHAPTER 6

Laying the final cornerstone of profit

Build your team

This is No. 9 from the strategic sales plan elements. Businesses are built by teams – mostly. Larger companies have long managed their salespeople differently from other employees, placing more emphasis on individual performance than on teamwork. While there is some evidence that a high-performing sales team will outperform a group of high-performing sales individuals, it is not so clear that all businesses would benefit from a true team-based approach to their salesforce.

What is a high-performance team? In his book *The Wisdom of Teams: Creating the High-Performance Organization*, Jon Katzenbach wrote this definition:

> A team is a small number of people with complementary skills who are committed to a common purpose, performance goals, and approach for which they hold themselves mutually accountable.

Jon argues that many so-called teams are not genuine teams and cannot attain the level of performance that real teams can.

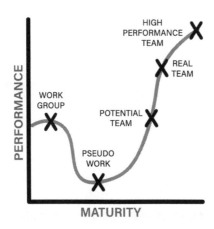

In our sales team, we may fantasise about having a collection of high-performing individuals. Of course, we want people who can maximise the results of their own activities. Will those individual high performers, those superstars, fit into a real team? To become a team requires individuals to make sacrifices for the team. All members of that team must put the collective needs of the group ahead of their individual interests. Are we going to get those attitudes and behaviours in a sales team? Or will we get, "Once I hit my quota, then maybe if I have some extra time, I'll help you"? Are you as the boss going to incentivise and reward person A for taking time away from their patch to help person B close a deal? Are you going to change individual targets and rewards and give only equal-share team bonuses?

Many businesses describe the sales department as a sales team. In truth, they are not a team. They don't operate as a team. The skill sets across the group of people are very similar rather than complementary, the goals are individual goals rather than team goals and the reward and recognition systems are designed to motivate individual performance.

Yes, we want people with similar values and attitudes who can collaborate as and when required. We do need salespeople who will network inside their own company and tap into the skill, experience and knowledge around them. There is a need for everyone to get along and to be supportive of others and the group. We need people who will, occasionally, go out of their way for the greater good. That does not mean you have to create more than an effective working group.

If you are serious about creating a genuine high-performance team, please read *The Five Dysfunctions of a Team: A Leadership Fable* by Patrick Lencioni first, as well as *The Wisdom of Teams: Creating the High-Performance Organization*, mentioned above.

Your working group is, of course, made up by individuals. Hopefully, the majority of them are an ideal fit for the role and your company.

The ideal salesperson

What is the makeup of an ideal salesperson? Would it be someone who could successfully and consistently sell value rather than price and navigate their way through the complexity of human relationships? Would they be able to build long-term, worthwhile client relationships while not taking their eye off the need to make profitable sales?

A good salesperson would do all that and more. Great salespeople have more than just a collection of skills, such as being confident when approaching people they don't know, or an ability to ask open questions; rather they exude certain attitudes, qualities, behaviours and habits that put them heads above the rest. Constantly working to develop the traits of a great salesperson yourself is part of the Profit Secret as is recruiting people who already demonstrate those traits.

Character traits of great salespeople

Conscientiousness. A study published in an American Psychological Association journal found that the men and women who scored highly in conscientiousness achieved more sales and were rated more highly by their bosses than those with lower conscientiousness scores. If they are conscientious, they will prepare for meetings, make the required number of phone calls or drop-ins, fill in the CRM and follow up on their promises.

Competitiveness. Steve W Martin, who teaches sales strategy at the University of Southern California Marshall School of Business, tested thousands of top business-to-business salespeople. He showed that 84% of top performers had a high achievement orientation. "They are fixated on achieving goals," he wrote, "and continuously measure their performance in comparison to their goals." Martin also found that 85% of top salespeople had played a sport at school. Someone who is competing with the best in their peer group and, more importantly, themselves has an inbuilt desire to be better every day.

Enthusiasm. What else is as contagious as enthusiasm? Have you ever been with someone who is very enthusiastic? How long does it take for some of their energy to rub off on you? Sales has often been called 'the transfer of enthusiasm'. The more enthusiastic and convinced you are about what you are selling, the more contagious this enthusiasm is and the more your customer picks it up and acts on it.

To be enthusiastic you must like yourself, what you do and your clients. That authentic enthusiasm oozes out of every pore of your body. Your prospects and customers can feel it. As a result, people want to buy from you, repeatedly, and recommend you to their friends.

Enthusiastic people tend to have a general sense of gratitude about their current and past life, including some of the challenges they have faced. They also have a positive expectation about every opportunity. This positive expectation creates a love of trying, attempting, and learning as you go – Ready, Fire, Aim. This adds a dynamic hope-filled drive to the resilience that is essential for great accomplishment. Both the positive and negative salesperson live in a land of self-fulfilling prophecies.

Persistence and handling of rejection. Anyone who has worked their way through a batch of 80 cold calls during a day without making a single appointment has had to face rejection and yet carry on. It may take the average salesperson 118 cold calls to make one appointment. If they take the 117 rejections personally, they develop call reluctance and may never get to that appointment-making call. This may well be the biggest cause of failure in sales.

The persistent salesperson has tenacity, patience and resilience, they recognise that the word 'no' means 'no today' rather than 'no never'. How many salespeople follow up after the first 'no' from a prospect? I've seen some scary statistics, for example, that 44% of salespeople give up after the first 'no'. I cannot find the evidence to support that claim. What we do know is that fewer salespeople go back after the first 'no' than those who don't. Successful salespeople go back.

My recommendation is to go back at least five times and stop after the ninth. After nine attempts put the prospect's details back in the marketing pot. They are not ready to buy; they probably are not even looking. Use marketing to whet their appetite, to warm them up. Marketing is designed to get people to look; sales is meant for people who are nearer that point of being ready to buy.

Why bother going back? Because everyone is likely to experience some changes over time. No business is static, machines break down, suppliers make mistakes, people change jobs and some people do change their mind. Only the persistent and patient salesperson is ever going to work at the prospect's pace and discover the truth about that for themselves.

Curiosity. Someone who is insatiably curious is simply going to ask more questions, to learn the facts of the situation and to understand the implication or consequences of what is happening. In various studies, high-performing salespeople typically ask twice as many questions than salespeople whose results are average or below. If someone is genuinely curious, they are also likely to be excellent listeners. What better than a salesperson who can discover and understand a prospect's true pain points and their real reasons for investing in a solution.

Quick thinking and intuition. A great salesperson will approach any situation – from a phone call, to a product demonstration to handling an objection – with a clear objective in mind and well-tried conversation plan. Yet we know the most reliable thing about conversations with prospects is that you are going to come across something different and even surprising at times. Not only do great salespeople have a high degree of self-awareness, they also have behavioural flexibility. They know when it is time to deviate from the script. They can also see forward and consider where, how and why price resistance may show itself later in the process with each prospect. They can respond in the moment, adapt on the spot, and feel comfortable saying or doing something different.

Situational dominance. This a personal interaction strategy by which the prospect accepts the salesperson's right to lead the conversation, ask questions and gain deep insights into the prospect's problems. Prospects intuitively accept that the salesperson has the credibility and the authority to make recommendations. A situationally dominant salesperson can be relaxed in any prospect's office, whether that prospect is a global chief executive or a one-man band. They can set the agenda, guide the conversation, confidently ask probing questions and freely share their knowledge and opinions.

What do top salespeople know?

When recruiting and training a new salesperson, it is very useful to work out what the most important things are that a salesperson should know, then screen the applicants against that knowledge. I've asked thousands of people that question in sales training programmes across the world. Here is a list of 10 things I often get back.

Top 10 things to know:

- How to write, speak and present professionally.
- How to dress appropriately.
- Your industry or marketplace, your company, products and/or services.
- Your buyers' personas – the full description of their world, their pain points or problems, their needs and buying processes and their main reference points.

- Some psychology – how people tick, how to influence and persuade and when to walk away.

- Your goals, targets, your sales process.

- Your existing customers and the prospects in your current pipeline.

- Your terms and conditions, your refund or cancellation policies.

- Your competition.

- A rounded general knowledge so you can hold a conversation about more than just left-handed widgets.

That is certainly not an exhaustive list, just enough to point you in the right direction when you create your own list.

The most important skills

Another question I often ask during a sales training session is, "What are the most important skills a great salesperson excels at?" Here is a sample of some of the great answers I've been given over the years.

- Can easily establish rapport and trust with anyone and especially the prospect or customer personalising all their interactions.

- Asking great open questions that reveal needs and pain points, and their consequences.

- Practise active listening, acting on or adapting to what is said, as well as having a good memory of who said what and when.

- Ability to communicate succinctly, clearly and persuasively, and to tell compelling stories or explain things well – one-to-one or as a public speaker.

- Use psychology to engage, enthuse, motivate and persuade the buyer.

- Are great copywriters.

- Help prospects achieve their next steps and solve their problems.

- Tie their time management, personal organisation and daily activities to achieving goals and key performance indicators (KPIs).

- Manage their pipeline to consistently achieve above target results.

- Handle objections and questions well and can close over 50% of sales opportunities.

In selecting the 10 most important skills for you and your company, you will of course rate some skills as less important. That doesn't mean that they are not important, merely that some skills are more essential in your view. If you forced me to narrow this list of skills down to the essential few then I'd say:

- Relationship building

- Questioning skills

- Listening skills

- Planning skills

Why is relationship building so important? Because people don't care about what you know until they know how much you care. Their head is unlikely to listen until their heart has heard. The best salespeople really care about people and are great at starting and developing relationships with a wide range of people. They gain rapport and trust authentically, quickly and easily.

Why are questioning and listening so important? Average salespeople score well in their ability to find out the basic facts and explain features and figures, but top performers dramatically outscore the rest when it comes to gathering information. In addition, how a salesperson collects information still distinguishes exceptional achievers from the rest of the pack.

Top performers ask more questions and better questions than the rest. As a result, they gain much better rapport, deeper trust and, of course, much more accurate and meaningful information. Their aim is to engage customers in the buying process with questions that require thoughtful answers, that stimulate curiosity and that reveal the customers' underlying needs and pain points, as well as the consequences of those – usually problematic and expensive consequences. Finding out those painful and costly consequences is part of the Profit Secret.

Alongside great questions come great active and passive listening skills.

Listening is generally split into two types: active and passive. To be effective with passive listening, you listen with an open mind, not a fixed blinkered point of view like a hammer looking to hit a nail. You communicate through your level of attention, slight facial expressions, subconscious body language and non-committal words. You face the speaker, make eye contact, lean in towards the speaker, have an open, relaxed posture, nod or shake your head. Non-committal words are sometimes used such as "Hmm," "I see," "Interesting," "Oh yeah," and so on. You are not interrupting, you are hardly interacting; they can see, hear and feel that you are listening.

Passive listening can be a challenge because your mind can move faster than your mouth, so it is quite possible for your mind to drift from the topic of discussion occasionally. The salesperson who loses attention is likely to lose the sale.

Active listening requires you to 'get inside' the speaker's head, so that you can understand the communication from their point of view. You work to understand what the speaker wants to communicate, you question, you probe. The two main skills involved in active listening are perception checking and paraphrasing.

Perception checking involves you asking questions about what they said; asking questions to explore further, to seek a deeper understanding, to clarify any doubts, to fill any gaps, or to build on what the speaker has said.

Paraphrasing is feeding back to the speaker what they have said in your own words and sometimes theirs. This invites the speaker to hear what you have understood. If your paraphrase does not sound quite right to them, they can clarify.

Why is planning so important? I'm sure we've all heard the expression, 'No one plans to fail – they simply fail to plan'. Well, great salespeople are inherently good thinkers and planners. They are good at looking at the big picture with their annual sales target and planning exactly how they intend to hit it, as well as looking at the little picture by planning their day and each call they make.

Top performers do not wait for anyone else to set annual or quarterly sales targets. They set their own goals. Typically, they will be more ambitious than any company target. Great salespeople break annual goals into quarterly goals, quarterly goals into monthly goals, monthly goals into weekly and then daily goals and tasks. They set objectives for each phone call and face-to-face meeting, usually phrased in the other person's self-interest. They plan thought-provoking questions that probe into the heart of the matter, collect the information they need and make the prospect think differently. They plan for the prospect having questions and objections, so they have case studies, compelling stories and video testimonials ready to show them. They plan reasonable next steps for the prospect to take on their decision-making journey. They help the prospect to plan the implementation after the big decision, and finally they work out a follow-up plan with the prospect, so that expectations are managed and met. Planning is part of the Profit Secret.

The most important habits

Officially a habit is a routine of behaviour, or a fixed way of thinking, which is repeated regularly and tends to occur subconsciously. Many of our habits are unconscious and we do not even realise we are doing them. They are a form of fast thinking; they consume minimal attention and very little energy.

Why are habits important? As Mahatma Gandhi put it, "Your beliefs become your thoughts. Your thoughts become your words. Your words become your actions. Your actions become your habits. Your habits become your values. Your values become your destiny."

Before Gandhi, Aristotle is reputed to have said, "We are what we repeatedly do. Excellence, then, is not an act, but a habit."

To become excellent at anything – sales, chess, or athletics – requires the cultivation of daily habits of excellence.

By a salesperson's habits I mean what do they do, pretty much every day. Well every working day. One part of the Profit Secret is that success comes from doing the right things, well enough and often enough. Some of those right things will be habits, performed well, every day – OK, almost every day. Taking time off is necessary for recharging batteries.

When I've asked delegates on sales training programmes, "What are the most important habits performed every day by excellent salespeople?" I get a variety of confused looks from the delegates.

Even people new to selling and those with relatively low levels of sales experience can tell me about a salesperson's knowledge, skills or attitudes.

The 'habit' question always throws people. What experienced salespeople and novices tend to produce in answer to the question is a repeat of the same skills or attitudes they listed before.

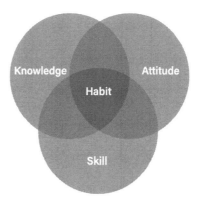

My theory about this is that routine has a bad name. Doing the same things over and over is boring, right? I want to be free to go with the flow, be spontaneous – you know that variety is the spice of life, isn't it? And remember most habits are developed unconsciously. Our dominant thoughts, even those that accidently dominate our mind, will dictate our behaviour; whatever we do often enough will become a habit. We develop habits by default, like it or not.

Is it worth intentionally developing a set of good habits to aid our success?

Yes. Having no routine or structure is so much more draining mentally, physically and emotionally than having a routine could ever be. And those habits are likely to be the foundation of greater success.

William James, a leading philosopher and psychologist (1842–1910), said,

"The more of the details of our daily life we can hand over to the effortless custody of automatism, the more our higher powers of mind will be set free for their own proper work."

Wood & Drolet tested whether habits could improve, as well as derail, goal pursuit when people have limited willpower. Their paper, 'How do people adhere to goals when willpower is low? The profits (and pitfalls) of strong habits' was published in the *Journal of Personality and Social Psychology* in 2013.

Their five studies found that when willpower, or self-control and self-motivation are low, it is our habits that get us through. We are more likely to stick to our goals and achieve them, even though we don't feel great, if we have appropriate habits in place.

As Tynan explained in *Superhuman by Habit: A Guide to Becoming the Best Possible Version of Yourself, One Tiny Habit at a Time*, "Our willpower is limited, yet we rely on it every day to get our tasks done. Even if we build willpower slowly over time, it's never enough to reach all of our goals. The solution lies in habit creation, the method by which we transform hard tasks into easy ones, making them automatic and independent of our will power."

So, what would be the ideal routine for you? One that enriches, empowers and emboldens you. One that would give you a repeatable set of activities each day, each week, each month. Activities that when done well produce great results. Like a gymnast – a set routine they do not have to think about that produces near perfect 10 out of 10 performances time after time.

I recommend that you work out and write down what an ideal day, an ideal week and an ideal month would look like. Include some of the following habits in your ideal week.

> **Below are some initial daily habit suggestions. If you want to know more about each of them, visit www.bemoreeffective. com/theprofitsecret and if you are a first-time visitor, register and download the *Be More Effective Habit Guide.***

Some suggested habits

- Get up early, get ready, and have a get focused routine.
- Learn to disqualify. Hard.
- Conduct a daily sales team huddle.
- Sell to decision-makers and nobble their committee.
- Learn new ideas every day.
- Leverage introductions at and after every meeting.
- Never drink coffee or eat lunch alone.
- Track competitors; know more about them than anyone else.
- Rehearse lines until you are a natural, like a world-class actor.
- End each day by reviewing your performance and lessons learned.
- Say, "Thank you" emphatically.
- Maintain your energy and wellbeing.
- Be on time, deliver on time, start and finish on time.

Build your own sales competency model

Develop a sales competency matrix for yourself or your sales team by doing the following:

- List all the knowledge, attitudes, skills and habits you consider a salesperson needs to use to be successful in your industry.

Knowledge	Attitude	Skills	Habits

Separate each element (K A S H) out into its own table and describe the different levels of each of the items listed. (See example)

Skill	Basic	Intermediate	Advanced
Questioning	Asks questions focused on the prospect	Asks a good range of mixed, open and closed in the right proportion	Asks tactical questions to probe and analyse prospect pain points. Uses a structured set of questions well to guide the conversation

- Identify where a highly successful salesperson needs to be on each competency. Then work back to the basic level.

- Assess yourself honestly as to where you feel you are currently, then assess each person in your team.

- Identify the gaps between where you and your team are currently and the ideal.

- For each person, decide on one strength from all four sections (K A S H) to deploy better and one aspect from each section to improve. Now you have the beginnings of a personal development plan for yourself and each member of your team.

If you want to be more objective with the assessment, turn the above exercise into a 180-degree assessment by getting scores from five others who know each person well. The average of their peers' scores, or their customers' scores, compared to their own score and yours as their boss will be very revealing.

If you want more ideas and a blank worksheet to help you start working out your ideal salesperson, visit www.bemoreeffective. com/theprofitsecret and if you are a first-time visitor, register and download the *Ideal Salesperson Competency Worksheet*.

Recruitment methods

How do you find good or preferably great salespeople?

A well-written advertisement based on a precise job description, including the most important three goals, five KPIs and clear person description, would be a good start. There are some great online agencies, such as Webrecruit, which can ensure that your ad gets on to every job board for much lower fees than agencies typically charge. That does, however, mean filtering the applications yourself, running all the tests and conducting all the interviews – or paying someone you trust to do it for you. You may have a HR department or person that could help.

You could engage a specialist sales recruitment company or headhunter with a great reputation. A proven job placement service can save you a tremendous amount of time and a great many headaches.

You could go for a referral. Sometimes the best salespeople come from unexpected places. One client who ran a car dealership always asked the Snap-on Tools salesperson when he needed a new mechanic. Ask your clients, associates, your current sales team, colleagues in other departments and suppliers; they may well know exactly who you are looking for. Do remember to ask this qualifying question, "If you were in my position, would you hire the person you are referring to me?" And follow up with, "What evidence do you have that supports your view?" The answer to these questions may help dodge a bullet.

One answer is to be looking always, so that you are never caught without a talented person to bring in at the right time. Use social media to build connections and relationships with top talent; it is amazing just how much people share about their lives and work online. Keep an eye on Glassdoor and similar sites for information about your competitors and companies associated with your industry. When a company listed on Glassdoor receives a cluster of negative reviews, you can reach out to the people who are leaving those reviews. Unhappy employees and ex-employees may be looking for a better place to work. As with your ideal prospect, you can determine what your ideal salesperson looks like and where they probably hang out, online and offline.

Build relationships with the best salespeople, wherever you meet them. It is highly likely that you have, in the not too distant past, been through a sales funnel yourself when you were the buyer. Maybe you bought a car, some furniture, a computer or even a house. Whenever you buy something and were treated exceptionally well, consider ways to nurture a relationship with them. You don't know who they know. And it is just possible that they may one day be looking for a new opportunity.

> *"Get the right people on the bus, and the wrong people off it."*
>
> – Jim Collins (2001)

Jim Collins writes great books. In *Good to Great*, he coined the above phrase, and it is vital.

Most businesses are built by teams or at least working groups made up of great people. Top talent is an essential component of a top company. While you may be able to carry a few passengers, they will slow you down; trying to carry people sitting in the wrong seat on the bus, or those that insist on sitting the wrong way around, is lethal.

Even if you are a solo entrepreneur or a single salesperson, you need good people around to advise, support and challenge you; be they subcontractors, virtual assistants or suppliers. If you have people who are not pulling their weight or poor performers in your business, consider fair and reasonable ways to move them on or out. Get an enthusiastic, keen and hard-working person, even if they have less knowledge, and give them all the support they need to succeed. If you have advisers you don't trust or respect, replace them.

The framework of profit, the tools, systems and meetings

Tools and systems

No.10 from the strategic sales plan elements is Tools and Systems. It is vital to have things that support and simplify your activities. If a system or tool does not help you make more profitable sales, more often or more sustainably, you should question its value. With more than a thousand

Build Your Framework

suppliers of sales systems and tools, it is all too easy to make life more complicated and less productive for yourself and your sales team rather than the other way around.

How do you choose your sales tools?

Not all companies have the same needs and not all sales tools are created equal, so it is vital that you think and plan. Measure twice and cut once is easy advice to overlook. Start with your business goals. What blend of systems and tools would help you achieve them faster, more easily, or at a lower cost? What current problems would they solve? What could they automate or simplify? Once you have listed your objectives and prioritised your needs, then and only then start checking options, because only then can you evaluate the options they suggest. You do not want to be like a child in a sweet shop. Know what you need. And no, you cannot have them all. More tools and systems do not a better sales team make.

You want a set of tools that is easy to use and will produce the best, most integrated and most sustainable results. You want systems and tools that support, speed up, simplify and improve your sales process, improve everyone's focus and activity rate and in themselves take less time and effort than you currently use, not more. Tools that make data more accessible and actionable online, on the move and in the office. Systems that automate repetitive tasks and make hard tasks easier, if not error-free. Tools that make your sales process easier to follow, especially for new people. And without question make the reporting of your KPIs easier – daily, weekly, monthly, rolling quarterly – whenever, ideally.

Think of it this way:

- **Accelerate.** Can this tool or system help you accelerate your response or the buyer's journey in some way? Even the signing of contracts could be done far more efficiently with products such as those from DocuSign, for example.

- **Automate.** Can this tool or system be used to automate standard or repetitive activities?

- **Eliminate.** Can this tool or system help you eliminate work or reduce the time taken? Salespeople can easily spend a third of their time finding current content or creating new content to send to prospects, much of it duplicates. How could a system or tool eliminate duplication of work and files?

- **Assist.** Can you use systems to directly update your CRM with relevant information about a new lead?

The main types of tools and systems to consider

If I were to list the '10 best tools and systems' in this book, by the time you read it the list would be out of date. More valuable advice would be to reflect on the most essential types of systems to investigate. Some of these can be found in enhanced CRM systems or as third-party application that will integrate with your CRM:

- LinkedIn Sales Navigator
- Lead handling and prospecting
- Analytics and reporting
- Document management
- Invoicing software

- Inventory and order management software
- Email management, automation and integration
- Video or webcast meeting system
- Survey tools
- Personalised video creation app
- Calendar app that prospects and customers can access easily

Sales productivity is increasingly important in all industries. To make highly profitable sales and grow your results sustainably, you must be able to respond quickly in a consistent, repeatable and scalable fashion. Unless you maximise the use and integration of the systems and tools available, actual selling time will decrease.

True selling time is when you and your salespeople are ear-to-ear or toe-to-toe with prospects and customers. For most businesses, core selling activity time generally represents less than 30% of a sales rep's day. One part of the Profit Secret is to increase face-to-face time, or phone time, in other words true human-to-human (H2H) selling time. Systems and tools can help you do that. If H2H time increases, so will sales.

Metrics

No.11 from the strategic sales plan elements is Metrics and we covered the most important measures of performance in the current state analysis earlier in this book.

Knowing where you are against plan, against the last period – be that a year or a quarter or a month – is vital for focus and for motivation. With a proper KPI measurement strategy set in place, you'll have more control over your results and your growth.

It is much harder to improve what is not being measured, analysed and fed back.

Use the most important measures to create a visual sales dashboard.

Turn numbers into informative graphs. Graphs and charts can visually add a narrative to the numbers without lots of words. A well-constructed, real-time dashboard can give a quick insightful overview of performance and suggest a series of next actions to move things forward. It can tell you whether the right things are being done, well enough and often enough – or not.

Creating a visual representation of your up-to-date pipeline to educate and engage the whole of your sales team or colleagues would be a very smart thing to do. The truth sets us free. Hard, visual data can challenge and inspire people to improve.

Budgeting

No. 12 from the strategic sales plan elements is Budgeting, Reports, Meetings and Sprint Plans. Let start with Budgeting. Some business owners run their businesses in a relaxed way and may not see the need to budget. Be careful. Sales is vanity, profit is sanity and cash is king. Settings budgets is a vital part of planning for success. Even if you have only your wages and commission to consider, you do still want to be paid, don't you? When planning for your business's future, for your growth, you will need to fund your plans. Working out the costs and when those costs will need to be paid is the most effective way to control your cashflow. Measure twice, cut once. Planning will enable you to know when you can and cannot invest in new opportunities, people and equipment.

To create your budget, begin by asking these questions:

- What are the projected sales for the budget period? For budgeting purposes, you could set test two figures: your real goal and a lower target. This will help you test the tolerance in your cashflow.

- What are the direct costs of sales, i.e. costs of materials, components or subcontractors to make the product or supply the service? What happens if these go up or down by 2%, 5% or 10%?

- What are the fixed costs or overheads? You should break down the fixed costs and overheads by type.

Your budgeting, as part of your sales and business plan, should help establish the relevant links between the growth in sales, the increased cost of those sales, as well as when and by how much fixed costs and overheads will change.

Once you've got figures for income and expenditure, you can work out how much money you're making. There is the profit we've been talking about. You can also look at your sales margin or your pricing, as well as your fixed and variable costs, to work out ways to improve the profit.

Cashflow statement

Cashflow is the essential pulse of a business. The flow is money coming in from clients and going out to cover the costs.

A budget tells you what you want to spend money on. The cashflow statement sets out the various inflows and outflows of money through a company over time. It shows you how much cash you have on hand in the bank, how much you are owed by customers and how much you owe others and will need to pay at some point, including any loans or borrowings.

The cashflow statement can tell you when there may be a pinch point. You should be able to see three to six months ahead if you are going to have a problem, which should hopefully give you enough time to do something about it.

What is a budget report then?

You may also need to produce a budget report each month or quarter. A budget report gives a moment-in-time snapshot of the financial performance of a business compared to what you forecast in your sales targets and original budget.

Producing a budget report will encourage you to review your budget regularly. If your sales and therefore your business are growing profitably, as desired, you may need to revise your budget. Using an up-to-date budget will give you confidence and enable you to be flexible in your approach to managing your cashflow to support the achievement of your goals.

Once armed with this knowledge, you are better placed to do two things more effectively as a salesperson:

1. Develop a firmer belief that you offer outstanding value and help you in your efforts to develop more resilience in defending and justifying your price.

2. Learning more about business costs and budgeting will help you cultivate more carefully framed questions to ask prospects. This training may help you be more effective at uncovering prospect needs in a way that allows you to sell at a higher price.

Meetings

What are the essential meetings required to enhance the alignment of effort towards the key goals and improve accountability?

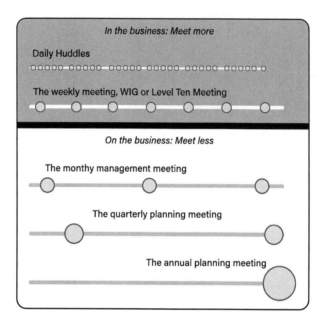

Daily huddles

Daily sales team huddles are essential. This meeting should be short, 10–15 minutes; its brevity keeps everyone focused on the here and now while its frequency ensures progress. Same time every day, same place. Ideally around a kanban board, which visualises each person's work-in-progress (to do, doing, done). There are only three items on the agenda:

1. Most important key activities, meetings or decisions for each person over the next 24 hours. Look for potential synergies or conflict.

...at opportunity to include everyone in a reflective,
...enquiry about the previous quarter before creating the
...'s activity or sprint plan. The senior team can introduce
...arter's most important goals – ideally just three or
...through a facilitated interactive session, everyone can
...ideas on how those goals can be achieved. If this is
...ell, even the individual quarterly plans can be written
...rafted during the session, making the session incredibly
...d time-efficient.

...le may stay for only part of the day, to allow the
...agers to deal with more strategic, sensitive, or long-
...s, including decisions about an individual salesperson's
...rmance.

...want to retain your top talent, the A players. One way
... is quarterly performance reviews. Slow performance
...nt by the leader will unsettle the A players, so act
...o identify and resolve underperformance. B players
...y engaged in coaching or training in or around these
...meetings to lift their performance. C players are moved
...rtive way to roles where they may have a better chance of
...A or B players.

...al planning meeting

...h year an annual meeting replaces a quarterly one. This
...similar agenda with the addition of external speakers
...formal training sessions. For the senior team it may be
...d by an additional strategy session of one or two days.

...al meetings

...e sales team and company meetings, the sales manager
...have individual one-to-one sessions with each salesperson.
...ern and length of one-to-one meetings is similar to that
...meetings – daily, weekly, monthly, quarterly and annually.

2. What are my daily scores? Key daily measures that each person monitors plus any additional major daily company metric. Look for potential patterns or trends.

3. Where am I stuck? Anyone not 'stuck' every few days is not telling the whole truth. Follow up on any barriers or problems outside the huddle and solve them.

Remember, you can conduct huddles, as with any meeting, by Skype or Zoom or even the good old phone conference.

The weekly meeting, WIG or Level 10 meeting

Weekly discussions about progress on the quarterly priorities are a vital part of the Profit Secret. Using a standard agenda for these significantly improves focus and outcomes. Two good versions are the 'wildly important goal' (WIG) from Covey which has a 20–30-minute format or the 60-minute Level 10 meeting format. The name comes from the last item on the standing agenda where everyone scores the meeting out of 10. Any score of eight or below must be explained so that the quality of future meetings can be improved.

The daily huddle is for everyday issues and updates that pop up. You go in, share, align and you are out. The issues get dealt with afterwards by the relevant people. The weekly meeting follows a different format; it is not about addressing issues that have been allowed to accumulate over the week – most of them you should tackle as they are noticed. It is about making progress on the most important goals, more quickly and more confidently. It is about clearing the path to the future.

Held the same day and time each week, they form a key part of the cadence of alignment and accountability. They are action-oriented meetings focused on addressing key issues and on making decisions to move you towards your key goals, rather than spending time gazing in the rear-view mirror.

Each person can report on their key metrics and progress towards their goals. Each person can celebrate their victories and lessons learned. More importantly, each person must contribute to making faster progress. What problems need to be solved, what decisions need to be made, what risks managed? What questions answered? This is still centred around working in the business, making things happen now or at least next week.

Even if the team decides to work on and resolve one or two issues, that is a great result, provided that what is decided as an outcome means each person, or key players in the team, or the whole team can make faster progress the following week.

The meeting ends with each declaring one or two things they can personally do next week to make progress. Who is doing what and by when must be made clear to all. The team is making shared commitments and inviting mutual accountability. Last, as mentioned above, each person scores the meeting out of 10.

It is a good idea to schedule the meeting so it finishes at a break or lunchtime, as this aids a timely finish and social interaction afterwards.

> Do you want to make your meetings magic?! Visit w w w. bemoreeffective.com/theprofitsecret and if you are a first-time visitor, register and download the *Be More Effective Meeting Guide* and the *Meeting Planner*.

The monthly management meeting

This should be a half-day meeting, same day and time each month, in which the team and any senior decision-makers come together to assess progress, learn and collaboratively address one or two big issues with the aim of making progress faster, more confidently and more easily. It is about clearing the path to the future, working **on** the business, not working **in** it.

Every meeting should deliver value, and share your agenda in plenty of can do their own planning and pre be reporting on their own results a and foster transparency along wit course, there is going to be an update and a review of the pipeline.

Do allocate time to sharing success performance with awards and pra element, some participation that n knowledge or skills.

Identify one or two big issues that are the key goals; select only topics that ap which everyone can contribute intellig

Wrap things up positively, on time, lead end of the working day. Never overrun made a clear personal commitment to t a specific action in the following week o and by when?" is a key phrase for the cl of the meeting. Score the meeting out o

The quarterly planning meeting

Once each quarter, replace the monthly quarterly meeting format. The purpose meeting is to review results and perfo quarter and most importantly plan your along with some education, training or te

This could be a four- to eight-hour event next four meetings scheduled in everyone'

Yes, celebrate, give out awards and appropri big topics of the event must be the review

It is a gre appreciativ next quarte the next four. Then, contribute managed or at least valuable a

Some peo senior ma term topi underperf

Ideally yo to do tha managem quickly t are active quarterly in a supp becoming

The ann

Once ea follows or more proceede

Individ

Alongsi needs tc The pat of team

If you are a single salesperson or solo entrepreneur, find yourself a peer, associate or a friend, someone you respect and who understands the world of business if not the world of sales and have a meeting with them. Peer-to-peer coaching can be highly effective. Over my own career, I've had more time with a peer coach than a paid professional coach and both have been equally effective at keeping me focused, encouraging me to learn and holding me to account.

All one-to-one meetings give the sales manager and the salesperson time for reflection, learning and goal-setting, as well as an opportunity for both to raise any concerns or problems that may be slowing the progress to activity targets or results.

All meetings can follow a variation of the GROW coaching model. If you are not familiar with the GROW model, read *Coaching For Performance: Growing People, Performance and Purpose* by John Whitmore, who was a pioneer of the executive coaching industry.

GROW stands for:

- **Goal** – for this meeting as well as the goals you have been working on
- **Reality** – the current numbers, what is going well now and what is not
- **Options** – the brainstorming of ideas to improve performance
- **Will** – an action plan that both parties are committed to

All coaching sessions are based on the coach asking insightful questions as well as listening very well. This will aid self-discovery in the salesperson. The questions are a form of appreciative inquiry looking to create better clarity and alignment to goals; enhance learning from activity and results; encourage creativity and performance improvement; as well as enhancing commitment and accountability to a small number of actions and plans.

As a manager, while you do have to use part of each individual meeting to go over sales numbers, your main responsibility is to foster professional development for your salesperson, ensure they have everything they need to excel in your organisation and clear their path to success.

Weekly one-to-one meetings

These can be done using Zoom or Skype or Teams so that you are still face-to-face, even if not in the same location. They can be short meetings, just 15–20 minutes, and tightly focused on last week and the coming week. Link the salesperson's goals to their pipeline management and their activity – how well they are balancing time and effort between:

- prospects with deals closest to closure
- the hottest fresh leads
- their best customers, to protect and develop along with collecting referrals
- accounts whose sales volumes are slipping
- projects or deals that have been kicked into the red zone – delayed or stalled by factors outside your control
- their catapults – a small number of prospects who could produce at least 10 times the typical average annual order value, or could become a top 4% customer

One part of the Profit Secret is: doing the right things well enough and often enough. These critical parts of the pipeline help define the right thing – the prospects and deals across the different aspects of the pipeline that they need to focus on.

Review the progress made and barriers to progress found from last week, learn some lessons and plan the coming week. Determine a small number of key tasks or actions, up to four, that are highly likely to speed up progress in the coming week and to which the salesperson is wholeheartedly committed. Help them plan an ideal week.

Monthly one-to-one meetings

These meetings are best conducted face-to-face, or by Zoom or Skype or Teams if necessary, and should take 45–60 minutes. They cover a more in-depth review of the previous month, the pipeline, the activity and results as part of the GROW structure to the meeting. An appreciative inquiry approach (i.e. what is working) will keep things positive and facilitate learning and the development of better options, plans and actions for the coming month.

With the extra time you can invest in more mentoring or training elements to improve knowledge and skills. Alternatively, you can work together on a specific proposal or the salesperson's single most important prospect or project. The meeting must add real and significant value.

As part of the monthly session you will, of course, determine a small number of key tasks or actions, up to four, that are highly likely to speed up progress in the coming month and to which the salesperson is wholeheartedly committed. It must help them plan an ideal month.

Quarterly one-to-one meetings

Annual appraisals do not work. A far more effective performance management approach is to use quarterly coaching sessions alongside the weekly and monthly sessions. These quarterly sessions should take an hour or two, conducted face-to-face or by video. While the quarterly session also follows the GROW structure and appreciative inquiry approach, there is a greater focus on understanding your salesperson's motivators, drivers and thinking style to foster personal development alongside skill development.

Knowing which motivators and drivers are more important to each person in your team is key. Motivational mapping (www.motivationalmaps.com) is a simple, inexpensive and insightful process. *Mapping Motivation: Unlocking the Key to Employee Energy and Engagement* by James Sale is also a great resource for any manager and coach.

On a simpler level, understanding that a salesperson may rightly be more worried about the illness of a loved one than about a drop in their results is key. With more time in the quarterly one-to-one meeting you can connect more with the whole person.

You can also take the time to evaluate and sharpen their critical thinking skills. Remember that how a person views an opportunity, sizes up a potential prospect or thinks about one type of objection matters. How we see things is at least half of the problem, if not the whole problem.

The longer meeting can also provide the space to look for new opportunities for the person, not just skill development but career development too. Not simply account development – more how they can take their performance and approach to a new level.

As part of the quarterly session you will, of course, review the previous quarter, plan the next quarter and determine a small number of key tasks or actions, up to four, that are highly likely to speed up progress in the coming quarter and to which the salesperson is wholeheartedly committed. It must help them plan an ideal quarter.

Sprint plans

This agile planning tool can be used at a business, team and individual level, cascading up and down between the three levels. There are different formats of this tool, sometimes referred to as a SOAP (strategy on a page), from different gurus.

If we consider the journey we've taken in this book through a strategic sales plan, it will be obvious that such a comprehensive and reasonably lengthy document is not going to be something we carry around and read every day.

We can, however, condense it so that it fits on one page. The major components of a business sprint plan are:

1. The single most important goal for the business over the next year. Often a turnover or gross profit goal. Sometimes called a wildly important goal (WIG).

2. Three or four supporting one-year goals drawn from the balanced scorecard model (sales goals, customer satisfaction goals, internal improvement goals, innovation goals)

3. Three major goals for the next quarter.

4. Three major goals for the next month.

5. Three to five key daily activity measures or KPIs that can determine the health of the business and tell us whether we collectively have had a good day or not.

The above structure can also be used for team sprint plans.

Individual sprint plans need have only:

1. The single most important goal for the person; their most important contribution to the company WIG.

2. Three major goals for the next quarter.

3. Three major goals for the next month.

4. Three to five key daily activity measures or KPIs that can tell that person whether they have had a good day or not.

The sprint plans are updated each month and rewritten each quarter. They are a significant document to review in any business or team meeting, as well as in everyone's one-to-one sessions. The salesperson's pipeline, the sprint plan and the kanban board are three important planning and accountability tools. Why are all these meetings and tools part of the Profit Secret? Because even though they are amazingly powerful, few sales managers and salespeople use them.

Summary

We have completed our journey through the strategic sales plan that we started in Chapter 4. In terms of the value house sales model, we know where to build our house, we have dug good foundations, laid the cornerstones and created the framework. So, we can now start building above ground.

CHAPTER 8

The internal
building blocks
of profit

In this chapter we will look at several internal building blocks we want to have in place. Bricks that will provide shape, rigidity and safety.

Building block one – our own mentality

One of the biggest myths in sales, even today, is that the client always wants and buys at the lowest price. This myth is so strong and powerful that many salespeople are mesmerised and think that the myth is true. Such a mindset changes their approach to selling and makes selling at a high margin impossible.

Are we as salespeople to blame for the widespread belief in this myth?

In *91 Mistakes Smart Salespeople Make*, Tim Connor quotes a survey where price was ranked the sixth priority of buyers, while most salespeople on the sales training programmes I've ever run rank price first. I did not fully believe Tim, so in 1996 I paid a student at Exeter University to call 600 buyers across the UK's south-west region and ask what factors they considered the most important when taking on a new supplier. Price came out 9th of 16 things. Now I believed Tim completely.

Who is making the bigger fuss about the selling price?

But here are some interesting truths...

First, only one company can be the cheapest. Do you want to be that company? I doubt it. Being the cheapest is rarely going to make you the most profitable. Operating at a gross margin of 9%, you need a huge turnover to make a net profit. Each industry is different – some alcohol companies have a 19% net profit ratio, while many advertising and computer companies quote 6%, and some online retail runs below 3%.

I am not keen on anything below 10% net profit ratio. And net profit is the profit I mean in the title the Profit Secret. While you may be in sales because you genuinely want to help people, I believe that is best served through a profitable organisation, even if it is one that chooses to reinvest all that profit back into helping others.

Second, very few buyers have price as the *only* factor that matters. If that were true, millions of companies would go out of business. Only the cheapest company in each field would get the sale. There would be no premium brands, no gold and silver – just aluminium or cardboard.

Third, many buying decisions are made, every day, in favour of the supplier with the highest price. If price were always the only factor, those sales would not happen. University studies from Harvard and California in the US to York in the UK suggests that only a small percentage of all buying decisions are based on logical reasons (price); the vast majority (over 80%) are made for emotional or subconscious reasons.

Great salespeople must deal with prospects pushing back on price. They develop a great deal of resilience to ensure the pain-solving aspects, the benefits, application advantages, value-adding elements, and the uncommon difference of their product or service shine brightly. They also remain vigilant to being misunderstood by the prospect and to misreading situations, questions or concerns raised by the prospect in a negative way.

Why would someone misread a situation negatively? That may be often down to something called a 'schema' (pronounced 'skeema').

Schemas can limit your sales success

What on earth is a 'schema' and how may it affect my sales success? I hear you ask. Well, it is not someone who is trying to come up with a scheme or be devious.

A schema can be thought of as a broad organising principle or mindset for interpreting information, which can sometimes involve a 'blind spot'. For salespeople, examples could include stereotyping people or situations, leading to false assumptions. In a sales situation, it can be the kiss of death. Let me share with you some assumptions salespeople nearly always make that can seriously damage their wealth!

Start here. What does this say? **Opportunitiesarenowhere**

- Many people see 'opportunities are nowhere'
- It can also read 'opportunities are now here'

It depends how you read it and that depends on your schema.

Assumptions, true or false?

The buyer knows what he wants.

Not true – most prospects do not know what they want. While they know what problems they have, it is the process of discussion through guided questioning that often reveals what they need and want.

The buyer is an expert on their problems.

Not true and a dangerous assumption. As Jeff Thull talks about in *Mastering the Complex Sale* and Mahan Khalsa in *Let's Get Real or Let's Not Play*, the salesperson or trusted adviser is the expert at thorough diagnosis. After all, your doctor would not allow you to diagnose yourself. Neither would your doctor prescribe a treatment until a proper diagnosis had been confirmed. Giving out a prescription before a proper diagnosis is called malpractice. The same is true in professional sales and in professional procurement.

You make a sale solely on price.

Not true. Have you ever paid more for something you could get cheaper? Come on, own up. Most of us have, if not everyone. Are you the cheapest in your marketplace? I pray not, for your sake. Do you have existing clients who buy from you knowing they could pay less with a competitor of yours? Of course you do. It is always about value and usually perceived value. Never about price.

The competition is all around you with better products and services.

Not true. Your competitor's marketing materials and sales activity will support such a proposition. Your prospects may suggest that, but often so they can strike a better deal with you. What is your source of power? Why *do* people buy from you? Why are your present customers buying from you? You have made some sales, right? You keep some customers? Even if you feel it was a bit of a fight. Well those people did not see your competition as much better. Remember what Walt Disney said, "I have been up against tough competition all my life. I wouldn't know how to get along without it."

Your only real weapon is cutting the price.

Not true. This is arguably the most dangerous myth of all because it kills your profitability. Be proud. Defend your product or service and your price. If you go into the meeting believing giving a discount is OK at the start, then you have already agreed to cut the price – it is now just a question of how much.

A choice you must make.

All of these are real and dangerous mindsets (schemas) that salespeople can have, and not one of them is true. Above all you need the mentality that positions you, in your own mind, as a salesperson with a product to sell that has a value to the prospect greater than price. You need to make a fair profit.

For the company you work for, or purely for yourself, you have an opportunity and a responsibility to cultivate and develop strategies that will enable you to forge strong relationships with your prospect so you can tune into how you can deliver real value-added solutions for them.

Please recognise that while yours may be a fiercely competitive marketplace, it is important not to lose sight as to what makes it competitive – you!

The hardest thing for your competition to duplicate is *you*. That is the biggest reality in today's market. Your products, services or solution are secondary to your knowledge, expertise and the difference you make for your customers. You can be the differentiator by:

- having a different attitude
- having a stronger work ethic
- working as though you have no clients yet
- treating each prospect and client as though they are your only client
- showing focused interest in others
- asking different, incisive questions
- adding more value
- going the extra mile

> *"It's your attitude not your aptitude that will always determine your altitude."*
>
> – Zig Ziglar

Focus on the positive and do not lose sight of your strengths – as a company, your product and you as a person. As Helen Keller (American author and the first deaf-blind person to attain a university degree) once said, "Keep your face to the sunshine and you cannot see the shadows."

When selling at a higher price to make a better profit, the first thing you may have to correct could be your own mentality that says you have to have (or be prepared to have) the lowest price. In the rare cases where it is true, you must ask whether you want to cultivate clients who are not prepared to value other factors. Remember, the single easiest thing your competition can copy is your price. When you win on price, you can lose on price.

Selling at a higher price is perfectly possible; indeed, many companies do it every day. To do it consistently and successfully comes from understanding the principles and mechanisms within the Profit Secret. They will assist you greatly in your sales effort and quest for profit.

As John Ruskin, leading English art critic and philanthropist of the Victorian era said,

"It's unwise to pay too much, but it's unwise to pay too little. When you pay too much, you lose a little money, that is all. When you pay too little, you sometimes lose everything, because the thing you bought was incapable of doing the thing you bought it to do. The common law of business balance prohibits from paying a little and getting a lot. It cannot be done. If you deal with the lowest bidder, it is well to add something for the risk you run. And if you do that, you will have enough to pay for something better."

Speed up your learning, fail fast

It is inevitable that you'll make mistakes. So, don't wait till you've figured out the 'perfect pitch' before moving forward. In sales, there is no failure – just lots of opportunities for experimentation, learning and growth. Show me a person who has not failed at anything, and I'll show you a person who has not achieved anything. Do not be frightened to try things, take risks and be adventurous.

Failure is one of the most fertile learning grounds we have access to. So, go out and do something; if you fail – learn. Fail fast and fail forwards. Accelerate your learning curve so you get through the apprentice stage as quickly as possible.

> If you want to explore mental models and the application of the paradoxical sales principles further, visit www.bemoreeffective.com/theprofitsecret and if you are a first-time visitor, register and download the *Mental Models Tip Sheet*.

 ## Building block two – forging differentiators

Differentiators are an important Profit Secret, because prospects are often very keen to tell us that there is no difference between us and our competition.

- "You are all the same."
- "Their proposal offers me pretty much the same."

Why would they say that? Well, it may appear to them that the other proposal does look the same and that is where you come in because a salesperson's job is to show that things are not equal.

Of course, they may also say it to 'flatten the ground', to show that everything is equal so in fact there is only *one* differentiator that they would like you to talk about. Guess what that is? Correct. Price.

To strengthen your case, how about developing better differentiators for your company and a better explanation of what you offer?

As Robert Bloom describes in *The Inside Advantage*, to grow your business profitably, you need to fully understand what you are offering customers in terms of the overall value and experience that you deliver to them – not the narrow transaction of buying a product, service or solution.

L'Oréal could describe itself as a perfume supplier because it does make and sell perfume. L'Oréal understands that it is in the business of helping women look and feel beautiful. This much larger mission is at the heart of the company's success because that mission drives everything it does and every message it shouts about to prospects and customers.

If you can crystallise an offering into a description of an overarching positive customer experience, and then hardwire it into every aspect of your business, profitable growth will be far more assured.

The uncommon advantage focuses on the value added to the client through the removal of their pain and the delivery of realised benefits, as well as the emotional appeal. It is the whole package that is so attractive to your clients and provides you with clear differences between you and your competitors. How do you uncover it?

First review your prospect avatar and the ideal prospect statement you created earlier in Chapter 3. You have completed that assignment and created your avatar, haven't you? If not, stop reading and do it now because you need those insights to help define and describe your uncommon advantage.

Create a table with three column headings: 'Product', 'Pain or Value' and 'Emotion'. In the first column, list every product and service offering, in detail rather than broad terms. Next to each item, define the pain this removes for the client, or the value it delivers. In the third column, outline the emotional assurance each aspect provides – or not. Be objective; consider asking clients and others for their input.

Once you have a comprehensive list, prioritise it.

- Which items do you own exclusively, in marketplace terms (not legal rights)?

- Which items are duplicates? Combine or eliminate elements not compelling enough to leave on their own.

- Which items are enduring? Time is far less likely to dim their appeal.

- Of the remaining options, which offerings will enable you to deliver a meaningful, beneficial and different experience at every customer touch point?

- Which one delivers the greatest emotional assurance to your most important customer needs and so ensures those key clients remain loyal to you and your company? This is likely to be your uncommon offering and ultimately your uncommon advantage, your Profit Secret.

Create your uncommon advantage statement

Craft a 15-word statement that defines the tangible benefits as well as the emotional customer experience you can deliver today and every day thereafter.

This cannot be blah-blah or marketing spin. That will not deliver sustained profitable growth. Most prospects can sense blah-blah at a hundred paces and that will simply undermine their confidence and trust in you.

While many people ask to see other companies' statements, these examples rarely excite and inspire people in the way they had hoped, because they did not sweat blood and tears to create them.

Whereas your own – now that is different. Here are two examples, along with the ideal prospect statement to provide context:

- Who? A UK decision-maker who must protect his people, products and profits at any cost.

- What? A dynamic team providing inspirational solutions of unrivalled quality to protect what matters most.

- Who? A business owner frustrated by slow growth who can afford an exceptional personal coaching experience.

- What? Consistent new client acquisition giving profitable business growth, through a motivated team coached by experts.

Build on what you already have

The idea is to inspire your customers by ensuring that they enjoy a positive experience at every touch point in their relationship with your company. This exercise may cause you to identify elements of your existing products and services that could be improved. Remember to enhance only those services your prospects and clients are genuinely interested in.

For instance, if you offer delivery within 10 miles, you could make it 25 miles. If you offer customer care and your competitors do the same, provide the service differently. You could perhaps offer a hotline number or a free smartphone app that they do not have – anything that makes accessing the service easier or quicker or makes it more responsive.

What could you offer that makes you different and that your prospect would value? Challenge what you do now and what you offer. Compare it to the prospect's typical pain and frustrations of doing business with companies in your industry. Compare yourself to your competitors and find a way to deliver the product or service and relieve their pain or frustrations better and faster.

If you want more help to guide you through developing your differentiators, visit www.bemoreeffective.com/theprofitsecret and if you are a first-time visitor, register and download the *Forging Differentiators Worksheet*.

Building block three – sales process

Fundamental to selling at a higher price is having a sound prospect-focused sales process. Such a process should allow and facilitate the buyer's involvement, feedback and commitments from the very start.

The principle is very simple:

If you use a proactive process that the buyer is more than happy to engage in to serve their own interests, this should achieve three things:

Cohesion. The prospect works with you to the end of the process, when they would find it very difficult to make a decision solely on price, because the process itself has explored common ground on other factors they defined as important.

Isolate. The process itself will isolate, early on, any mismatch in the criteria being used for the basis of any decision.

Ownership. Having been involved in 'co-designing' the solution or major elements in your proposal, the prospect generally feels a sense of ownership, which helps reduce the likelihood of the business being given to a competitor.

A proactive, co-designed sales process can be synchronised with the prospect's buying process. You can learn to dance with your prospects; if they are doing a waltz, there is no point you doing a foxtrot. You need to learn their dance, or you will end up treading on their toes.

In many sales situations, you can be hooked into a reactive buying and sales process. The big risk is that the conversation will go straight to price. All too often it could look like this vicious circle.

Vicious circle

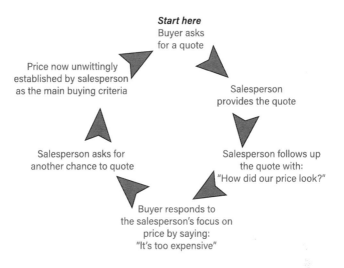

There are so many things wrong with this approach and very little of it helps when trying to sell a higher price.

1. The salesperson is reactive so will have much less control, if any.

2. Both parties use words such as 'quote' and 'cost' early on.

3. Both parties sidestep exploring problem identification, benefits gained and value added.

4. The salesperson puts themselves in a place where conceding on price will follow almost immediately once price pressure

is applied. Why? Because it has already come down to only one differentiator: price. Both parties believe the only game in town is drop the price or lose the order.

You are on the losing side the moment you agree to supply the quote requested because that stops both parties engaging in any meaningful dialogue.

What can you do about it?

Well, there are at least three things you can do:

1. **Be proactive.** The first thing you can do is to decide that from today, with any new prospect you will encourage them proactively to go through a diagnostic, co-designed, value-based sales process. In other words, you will aim to start at the beginning by:

   - building rapport
   - explaining to the prospect that to be able to offer them the best solution it would be to their advantage to explain some of the things that are important to them – their problem and needs, for instance
   - following accurate diagnosis, working with the prospect to co-design a solution matched specifically to their qualified pain, problem, needs and aspirations

   Working logically and reasonably through a process that enables them to buy effectively, dancing the same type of dance. At all times assuring them that their self-interests, problems and desires are of paramount importance to you. That you will offer them only a great solution that genuinely represents the best value to them.

2. **Break the circle.** Change the lead generation call to action. This may mean changing that 'Ask for a quote' call to action

on your website or e-shot to 'Find out more'. Ensure that the sales process starts with diagnosis, and that quotations cannot be sent without the context of their pain and the full value package as expressed in a sales letter or discussion document.

3. **Reverse engineer.** If you have lots of old and current enquiries from prospects who want you to send them quotations, you can decide that from today you will go back to each one and make a concerted effort to guide and steer them to the start of the process, asking appropriate questions to uncover their needs and frustrations. You could perhaps ask something like:

"I appreciate that you want the best value and our best possible price. To do that, it would help if you could clarify one or two things first – would that be OK?"

Remember though that when you do this, occasionally the 'odd' prospect may resist 'playing ball' with you. They may not want to be real or open, so they may choose to exit the process; most that do exit were probably price-checking.

The easiest thing any competitor can copy is your price. Some buyers will change suppliers for price, so if you secure a customer with that mindset and a competitor comes along and offers a lower price, what is that buyer going to do? Well, 90% of the time they are going to change suppliers again. Winning on price means you are vulnerable to losing on price.

A better, more strategic option that may make some of the price-checkers think is a nicely worded 'no bid' reply. It is worth replying and politely saying:

"Thank you for the opportunity to quote. Our expertise lies in a different value-based solution, which tends to solve x problems and generally adds more value because of Y. Without a more detailed discussion prior to any proposal, I cannot be certain of delivering the best value solution. If I am wrong and you are happy to have a detailed discussion, please do come back to me. Otherwise it would, in this case, be better or quicker for you to look to another supplier offering a price-based solution."

When selling on price, it is almost impossible to foster any kind of customer loyalty. Customer loyalty is highly prized and very difficult to buy. While customer loyalty can be bought, the currency required is not cash: it is value.

The buying process

It is best to consider the process that each party must go through. You start with understanding the buyer's process because any steps you use, as a salesperson, should always support the buyer through their process.

In his book *Major Account Sales Strategy*, Neil Rackham describes this generic buying process.

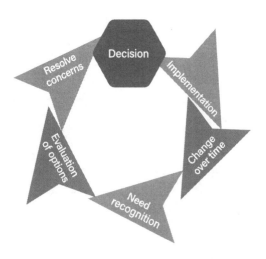

Recognition of needs

- Am I aware that I need to fix a problem? How big or important is it? Does it justify action now?

Evaluation of options

- Where can I find a solution to what I need? What options are available? Which are best for me? How do the features solve my problem? Who can supply this? What are the pluses and minuses of different options? Which criteria will I use to decide between the options? Price? Quality? Service? Functionality? Delivery? What vendor best meets the criteria?

Resolution of concerns

- What are the risks in moving forward? What could go wrong? Which vendor will be the safest option? What if I do nothing? Is that safer or more predictable? I do not want to make a mistake and be laughed at; no solution is a perfect fit. Which is the closest to what I think I need, in terms of time, cost and quality?

Decision

- Which is the best match to the decision-making criteria? Has the proposed solution been through all parts of the process? Do all the stakeholders agree on moving forward with the recommendation?

Implementation

- How do we get the greatest value from this decision? How quickly can we see results? What are the barriers and costs to a successful implementation? How do I resolve them?

Change over time

- Like it or not, things wear out, the world moves on, things go wrong.

The sales process

The success of any sales process is based on how well it uncovers the prospect's needs and wants while fulfilling the buyer's needs and aspirations with the specific matching benefits. The simplest sales process would be:

1. Find out what people want

2. Give it to them

That simplistic approach was developed into the AIDA four-stage process:

1. **Attention:** Opening the conversation and building rapport

2. **Interest:** Find out what people want by asking questions

3. **Desire:** Presenting relevant compelling desirable benefits

4. **Action:** Summarising and closing or getting commitment

The approach is attributed to American advertising and sales pioneer, Elias St Elmo Lewis. In 1898, Lewis created his AIDA funnel model to explain the mechanisms a purchaser of insurance went through for one of his clients. It became a model of personal selling. Lewis held that the most successful salespeople followed a hierarchical, four-layer process using the four cognitive phases that buyers follow when accepting a new idea or purchasing a new product.

Although there are many sales processes around today, the most successful have a structure that is based on building trust, developing long-term relationships and creating value-based solutions. They also recognise the buyer mentality and buyers' thought processes.

Below is the **value house sales process**.

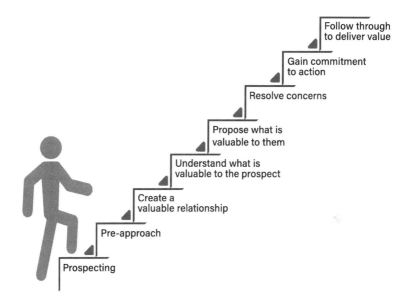

1. Prospecting

Prospecting refers to identifying and developing a list of potential clients. Salespeople can seek the names of prospects from a wide variety of sources including trade shows, commercially available databases or mailing lists, company sales records and in-house databases, website registrations, public records, referrals and directories.

Prospecting activities should be structured so that they identify only potential clients who fit the ideal profile and are able, willing and authorised to explore their company's needs and purchase a solution. Modern websites and email systems can go a long way in identifying visitors and automating the early stages of the qualification process.

2. Pre-approach

Before engaging in the personal selling process, sales professionals first analyse all the information they have available to them about a prospect to understand as much about them as possible. During this phase, salespeople work to anticipate the prospect's current needs, use of products and services and preferences. They also identify key decision-makers and influencers, and review any previous trading history. They plan questions to aid diagnosis of need and develop a likely pain hypothesis that includes the most likely concerns of the prospect to test. They may even reflect on the likely solutions. The sales professional also develops call objectives and a preliminary overall sales strategy for the early phases, keeping in mind that the strategy may have to be refined as more is discovered about the prospect.

3. Create a valuable relationship

This is the sales professional's initial contact with the prospect. They meet and greet the prospect, provide an introduction, establish the rapport that sets the foundation of the relationship, and ask open-ended questions to learn more about the prospect and their company. While the prospect talks and the salesperson listens effectively, trust is built. The prospect benefits from the attention, acceptance and approval of high-quality listening, and so their trust in the salesperson begins to develop. This phase also provides an opportunity to establish credibility on both sides, clarifying the roles of trusted adviser and the active, willing explorer of problems, needs, wants and requirements, otherwise known as the buyer.

4. Understand what is valuable to the prospect

Here is where the diagnosis happens. The salesperson asks a range of open questions, encouraging the prospect to elaborate on the details of their needs, leading to an understanding of the problems and their natural consequences. The prospect describes their goals and aspirations, their views on ideal solutions and how they or their organisation buy. The prospect does most of the talking in this stage, explaining and exploring key information, and more importantly, continuing to develop trust in the salesperson.

At the end of the understand step, before going on to the propose step, the sales professional finishes with a summary to check their understanding, offers a signpost of the potential solution and uses a trial closing question to test the appetite of the prospect.

Remember – the sale is made in the present pain, not the future gain. It is at this stage of the conversation, during the diagnosis, that the prospect makes up their mind to act. It is here the realisation is accepted that to carry on as they are now is not an option; it costs too much in time, effort and generally money. If enough trust has been built here, and there is acceptance of the need to change, it is time to explore solutions. If not, the buyer begins to reduce their level of engagement – even if it is hard for the salesperson to notice.

5. Propose what is valuable to them

During the presentation stage of the selling process, the sales professional tells a 'story' in a way that speaks directly to the prospect's identified needs and wants. A highly customised interactive presentation is the key component of this step. Demonstrations, audiovisual presentations or slide presentations may be incorporated at this stage, and this is usually when sales brochures or booklets are presented to the prospect. Top sales professionals encourage the prospect to continue doing much of the talking, even during the presentation.

This can easily be achieved by using the 'show, tell, ask' mechanism to ensure that the:

- features are shown (show)
- with the relevant pain and gain benefits described (tell)
- then the salesperson asks the prospect questions to explore the match to their declared needs, application requirements and desired benefits (ask)

Here the salesperson demonstrates that they *truly understand and care about the needs* of the prospect.

6. Resolve concerns

Professional salespeople elicit prospects' concerns, questions and objections. We know from the buying process discussed earlier that it is a natural step for the prospect to go through, so being part of that exploration is as valid as investigating their needs. First, you must fully understand their views before you can address, answer or overcome them. When prospects offer objections, it often signals that they need to hear more to make a fully informed decision. Uncovering objections, asking clarifying questions, and answering those concerns is a critical part of training for professional sellers.

7. Gain commitment to action

Closing is generally defined as the point where the salesperson asks for the order. There are many closing techniques. Top salespeople incorporate trial closing questions, such as, "What else would you like to know that may impact your decision to purchase?" or "How does that sound?"

After you have made a presentation and answered some questions from your prospect, be sure to ask more directly for the order. If the prospect gives an answer other than "Yes," it is your opportunity to identify objections and continue selling. Remember that sometimes you are closing on the prospect's next step in their buying process. It may not be appropriate to ask for the order yet because there are other hoops to jump through. Progress is the priority. Ask for their commitment to the next fair and reasonable step. Once that step has been taken, ask for commitment to the next fair and reasonable step. After a few such steps you will be asking for the actual order.

8. Follow through to deliver value

Follow-up is an often overlooked but important part of the selling process. After an order is received, it is in the best interests of everyone involved for the salesperson to follow up with the new customer to make sure the product or service was received in the proper condition, at the right time, installed properly, that comprehensive training was delivered, and that the entire process delighted the customer and the promised value has been realised. This is a critical step in ensuring the high level of customer satisfaction that builds long-term, profitable relationships. If the customer experienced any problems whatsoever, the sales professional can intervene to ensure 100% satisfaction. Diligent follow-up can also lead to uncovering new needs, additional purchases, testimonials and profitable referrals.

Each stage has its own protocol or guidelines. The chances of you successfully navigating to the next stage will be dependent on the degree to which you applied the principles and protocols of the previous stages.

The sales process must be customer-centric

If you are to sell value and avoid price resistance wherever possible, having an organised, systematic and repeatable approach is key to nurturing profitable customer relationships and scaling them. The process must recognise the buying process and the pace at which a decision-maker feels comfortable moving forward. Part of the Profit Secret is to ask yourself these questions at every stage of your sale process:

- How can I help this client get more of what he wants, through our process and service?

- Why is the next step obviously a sensible one for the prospect to take?

- What relevant value will they get in return, regardless of whether they become a customer in the end?

> **If you want to align your sales process more effectively with your prospect's decision-making process, visit www.bemoreeffective. com/theprofitsecret and if you are a first-time visitor, register and download the *Sales Process Worksheet*.**

CHAPTER 9

The external building blocks of profit

In this chapter we will look at several outward-facing or external building blocks we want to have in place, for instance:

- websites
- social media
- sales letters, literature, and direct mail
- electronic direct mail
- telemarketing and telesales

Building block four – your website

Having a website in place is vital today, whether your business is big or small. Most buyers start their search on the internet, so without a website your company would not exist for most prospects. A website is an essential and important building block in your value house – ideally one that shows up on the first page of search results because by 2019 fewer than 25% of people looked beyond that.

While this section of the book is not a thesis on website design, there are key aspects which matter most to prospects and therefore to salespeople because a website can help set and manage expectations for a prospect through their buying journey. Many of the ideas contain sales and marketing principles that can be used in plenty of other sales and customer service interactions.

Consider the following for your website and for much of your sales literature:

Know what your reader wants – make it personal. Write your website from the reader's point of view. You know who your ideal prospect is; you know the things that attract and interest them. You worked that out with your prospect avatar. What are your readers' concerns? Their problems? What do they value? What are their reference points? Which sources of authority do they look up to? What do they need to know to get them engaged? Write down all the questions, concerns and objections that you hear from your prospects and customers. Work out answers and put them on your website. Make them easy to find, engaging and simple to understand. Writing in a direct, 'I'm-talking-only-to-you' style will increase engagement and response.

Two types of readers. Half of what you need to have on your website, whether visible to the naked eye or hidden in code, is for search engines. Search engine optimisation (SEO) is a dark art generally left to specialists, still, they need you, as the salesperson, to tell them about the reader so they can feed the correct key search terms to the bots.

Motivate your reader to stay on the site. The home page, or a specific landing page, will be the first thing your reader sees. Get it wrong and they lose interest in two to four seconds. That means relevance and images. Relevance is key to grabbing attention. Thought-provoking statements about problems they recognise along with statements of the value they crave. Pain and gain will motivate the reader to stay on the site, to explore, to read. Great images or videos are vital; please do not use stock images – with good lighting and a good camera it is easy to take your own. You could even hire a professional. It would be worth it, because with a poor image, or worse – no dominant attractive, relevant image – that prospect is toast, gone and unlikely to come back.

Be careful to send out the right messages, not the wrong messages. In building your value house sales model, avoid provoking price resistance from the very beginning. It is so easy to do. For instance, I bet you have seen these statements on a whole host of websites:

- Special offer
- Buy three for the price of two
- Ask for a quote

When you mention anything of this kind, you make the reader think 'price'. Instead, write about value, the relief of their pain points and the delivery of the value they crave. Offer relevant information and access to special guides and white papers.

Start selling right away. Not everyone needs to know about every aspect of your product or service. Don't waste their time telling them about things they don't need to know. Address only your reader's needs, wants and wishes. Don't get carried away with your own interests. Provide the prospects with shortcuts to jump ahead to where they are in their buying process.

Ask for action. If you want your reader to respond – ask. One clear call to action. One thing they can do straight away. A simple response mechanism that is a logical and reasonable next step on their buying journey. It might be to download a brochure, or start a webchat, or enter their email address to get more specific information – and no, that does not include a quotation.

Link any listed features to the removal of pain and the delivery of benefits. Prospects care about getting rid of their pain and enjoying benefits. They rarely, if ever, care about features. If you must include a list of product features, add some phrases alongside them to describe the problems solved and benefits gained. It is more persuasive to show a feature with an image or diagram and describe the value statements next to the relevant image.

The more you can match the right pain and benefits to any features you mention, the more you keep the pain and gain in your prospect's mind. Building your value house sales model starts at the very beginning and continues all the way through the prospect's buying journey. That is part of the Profit Secret. It is never about the price, never. It is always about the value. The removal of pain and the delivery of benefits.

Give directions. Organise your website, and even your brochure, so that readers can find what they want, easily. Provide clear signposts or page titles or links throughout and make sure each one says, "Hey, pay attention to me!"

Keep the website fresh with new items of value. Adding relevant and helpful information to your website each week will help encourage the reader and search engine bots to return. Content marketing is cheaper and more effective than most people think.

 ## Building block five – social media

In today's digital world, every top salesperson needs a social media strategy to help develop customers and attract and convert prospects.

As with websites, if you do not have a profile on LinkedIn, then you won't be credible to many prospects, because that is where they look to establish the relevance and credibility of people new to their network. Social selling is contagious, whether positive or negative. Discovering that you are known by people they already trust helps. They can easily ask people they already know about you.

Is social media an effective business development channel?

Three statistics from 2019 demonstrate the effectiveness of social media:

- LinkedIn is the most effective social media platform at generating sales leads, with 65% of people surveyed having acquired a customer through the professional network, followed by company blogs (60%), Facebook (43%), and Twitter (40%).

- Most buyers (77%) say that they are more likely to buy from a company whose chief executive uses social media. Most employees (82%) say that they trust a company more when the chief executive and leadership team communicate via social media.

- Business-to-business companies with blogs generate an average of 67% more leads a month than non-blogging firms.

A strategic approach is to leverage content in social media as part of an overall objective to gain, nurture and retain customers. Social media can be used to listen to your target audience and then position credible, relevant and valued content as bait to attract narrowly targeted contacts in specific locations, industries and roles. While it is mostly a lead magnet, it is definitely an extremely useful one, with which a significant number of your ideal prospects and clients will engage.

How can you avoid wasting time?

The good news is that you do not have to create it all. You could use an app such as Refind to feed you highly filtered content links every day. In just 10 minutes, you could review the 20 links you've been sent and repost the best two or three on to different platforms. By introducing any post with a brief attention-getting statement, followed by a question, you will encourage readers to engage more with your post.

Including attractive images, compelling headlines and storytelling in your social media posts is an excellent way to keep your audience engaged and your brand memorable.

Use platforms such as Buffer or Hootsuite to enable you to post the same or similar content on multiple platforms in an automatic and pre-programmed way. That means you can easily post fresh content on each platform most days.

Frequent and consistent engagement on social media through the posting of relevant and insightful content does improve your chances of gaining mindshare. You start becoming familiar to prospects, and to prospects and customers alike you become someone who is worth knowing, possibly even a thought leader. Used well, social media can build your credibility, influence and reach, in a time-efficient, scalable and accessible way.

What about LinkedIn?

LinkedIn helps you engage with a community of 630 million business professionals (2019), four out of five being decision-makers at some level. Used effectively, it can drive connections and leads that are highly relevant to your business right into your lap. One client has worked his LinkedIn profile so well over the years that he has 30,000 industry connections, hundreds of views each day of his posts and more than enough leads to fuel growth of his business through a team of four salespeople. Who says social media doesn't work?

What are some LinkedIn tactics you can make good use of immediately?

- Write your LinkedIn profile and any other business profiles along AIDA lines, seeded with keyword phrases that prospects and clients would use. Your personal profile must be about you, not your company, even if you are the owner. In social selling, people buy people. Remember the call to action – what credible, free value can you offer to anyone appropriate who reaches out?

- Add branding, a banner, professional picture of you and a professional video or two.

- Four things to do every day on LinkedIn:
  - Check your connections' updates
  - Check group digests for opportunities to comment
  - Send connection requests to recent and upcoming meetings
  - Adopt a look and look back approach; if anyone looks at you, look at their profile for a reason to connect. Unless they look like timewasters, offer a connection

- Five things to do on LinkedIn before an important phone call or any face-to-face meeting:
  - Check your prospect's or client's profile for changes and events
  - See who else they have recently connected to
  - Review any shared connections
  - Check their groups for new comments from them or any trending issues
  - Read their recommendations, especially those they have written and given recently

Be prepared to take things offline. Social media and social selling is a great way to establish warm connections with prospects and clients. In the main it creates interest and warm leads. Once there has been some back-and-forth dialogue with someone on LinkedIn, it is easy to suggest a phone call or an email to deliver more information or to set up a meeting. If you have some pre-planned steps, some template emails or texts, some well-thought-out, ready-to-go materials, you are likely to have more success than by doing something random and different each time. Repeatable and scalable marketing and sales activities and habits are part of the Profit Secret.

> If you want the guide that I've created to help you generate awareness, connections and hot leads through social media, visit www.bemoreeffective.com/theprofitsecret and if you are a first-time visitor, register and download the free *Salesperson's Guide to Social Media.*

Building block six – sales letters, literature and direct mail

You may think about sending out letters or literature as part your prospecting activity. This may precede phone calls and meetings as a means of introduction or follow-on after the phone call or meeting to help make further progress with the opportunity.

Does direct mail still work?

In 1995, AOL and CompuServe showed up and started offering us all email addresses. Surely since then direct mail has died? Well, I am sorry to disappoint you – direct mail is still a vast market, with huge amounts spent each year. In the UK, it is estimated that more than 3 billion items of direct mail were delivered in 2018 and that most people receive 65 pieces a year. In the US, around 66 billion pieces are delivered each year, with the average household receiving between 450 and 800 pieces.

During 2018, the direct mail channels remained the third largest medium, in terms of advertising money spent, behind the internet and television. The Direct Mail Association (DMA) suggests, from members' feedback, that 51% of addressed direct mail is opened and of that, some 48% is read.

Another study by the DMA in 2016 showed the following opening rates or click-through rates:

- Unaddressed direct mail: 5.6%
- Social media: 0.6%
- Paid search: 0.5%

On sales conversion rates:

- Direct mail: 2.9%
- Email: 0.3%

So, it does work – still. And one of the reasons it works is that the medium of print is easier to understand for most people. One study found it takes 21% less cognitive effort – brainpower to you and me – to process and understand the message. That means your reader does not have to invest their precious time or brainpower in understanding your marketing message. More people get it – more easily than by email or social media channels, for instance.

Remember these 12 key strategies for your direct mail:

1. Use names and addresses – the opening rate is much better, even if you have to buy and clean a list first.

2. Getting the receiver to open the envelope is half the battle. Do something different and special with the envelope. It is pointless to spend money on what is on the inside and nothing on the outside.

3. Personalise the content – digital printing makes it easy to add names and other content into each direct mail piece. This alone can increase response rates by 30%.

4. Invest in good copywriting – if you got the receiver to open the envelope, you now have their attention. Make it credible, relevant, easy to understand and of value.

5. Make it uncommon – be creative. Do something that is uncommon in the message, packaging or printing. Ideally

all three. It is tough to be unique. The best goal is to be uncommon, to be different enough to stand out.

6. Incorporate images with the written content. Strong and compelling visual images alongside your written content to tell a story to the reader. You know the saying, 'One picture conveys a thousand words'.

7. *You* versus *I*. Writing things phrased in the other person's self-interest can make all the difference. Use 'you' *three* times more than 'I' or 'we'. This will force you to write more in their self-interest.

8. Make the reader feel something. Emotion is part of the Profit Secret. We typically buy with our emotions or feelings, then justify our decision with our thoughts and information.

9. Ethos, pathos, logos. Wherever possible, use three different angles in your communication. Follow one of the great leaders from ancient Greece, Socrates. He taught that a speaker's ability to persuade is based on how well the speaker appeals to their audience in three different areas: ethos (ethical appeals), pathos (emotional appeals), and logos (logical appeals). These areas form the rhetorical triangle. When you bring all three elements into your writing, you are highly likely to win more people over.

10. Consider using the AIDA formula as part of the copywriting.

11. Include a clear, single call to action.

12. Use direct mail in a mix with other methods, such as email marketing, telemarketing, social media and paid search. Include QR (Quick Response) codes or personalised URLs to specific landing pages. A recipient can then scan the code or visit the URL to reach a targeted landing page with personalised content.

Some common mistakes when writing new sales letters or literature

- Trying to sell everything and putting too much in
- Emphasising features rather than problems solved and benefits gained
- Being too focused on the seller (that is you, by the way)
- Too wordy
- Making price or discounts the main attraction

> If you want to read some good and poor examples of sales letters, including in-depth ideas on using AIDA to help you create better mailshots of your own, visit www.bemoreeffective.com/theprofitsecret and if you are a first-time visitor, register and download the *Introductory Sales Letter Guide.*

Building block seven – electronic direct mail

What about email marketing? Does that work? Surely with everyone under 30 using mobile phones and chatting on social media or via WhatsApp, email marketing must be dead?

In 2019, around 294 billion emails were sent each day, 55% of which were spam. Spammers receive on average one reply for every 12,500,000 emails sent – sadly enough to encourage them.

The largest proportion of email is some form of advertising. This includes promotional sales content that the recipient did not explicitly opt in to receive. This means your email is at risk of being lost in the noise, even if you have permission to send promotional emails to given recipients. Getting permission is vital or you risk wrecking your credibility before you even start. Please adhere to the General Data Protection Regulation (GDPR).

People are busy enough with real email messages, let alone spam and info-emails. By 2019, the average office worker received around 121 emails a day, including spam, and sent between 40 and 90 business emails daily. Getting the optimal frequency for your market is vital – ask 12 clients who you know love you. Test their feedback and find the best frequency for you, whether once a fortnight or once every six weeks. What matters is that people who want it will welcome it, provided the frequency is appropriate and the content credible, relevant and important to them.

Email, despite being talked about as a pain, remains popular, and not just with the over 30s. Even in 2019, 75% of teenagers had an email address. Most people are checking their email system more than 20 times a day and that appears to be on the rise; in part because more than 75% of us use our smartphones to receive and send emails. More than half of us even check our email before doing anything else online and before getting out of bed.

It would be crazy for any salesperson or business who wants to make a profit to ignore email as a channel to nurture new leads or stay in touch with clients.

Can email marketing help make you a profit? Yes. The evidence from various sources suggests that once people open the email and click through, the conversion to sales is good, and in many cases better than social media click-throughs. The email marketing industry claims to return £44 for every £1 spent.

Can emails help you sell at a higher margin? Yes. Research shows that people who buy products marketed through email spend 138% more than those who do not receive email offers.

Remember these key strategies when you use email:

- People have the power to get rid of the irrelevant emails that are cluttering up their inboxes, so use smart personalisation that goes beyond the addressee's first name and make your content more engaging.

- Make sure your content is targeted at the right audience. Relevance is a huge concern for us all. If it is not relevant, it will quickly be binned or blocked. Only one in seven of us believe that about half of all emails we receive are useful.

- Ensure that your campaigns are mobile-optimised. If they are not, you're missing out on a lot of potential connections, leads and sales. Emails that look poor on smartphones hurt your credibility.

- Create a lead magnet. This is something awesome and valued that you give away for free in exchange for an email address. It does not have to cost you anything to create; most lead magnets are digital materials, such as PDFs, MP3 audio files or videos that you can create yourself at minimal or no cost.

- Make your emails shareable. If your emails contain helpful information, your recipients will want to share them with others. By adding social share buttons to your emails, you can make it easier for people to share your content with their networks. This can help you increase awareness of your brand and social media links, expanding your reach online.

- Include videos or animated content. Email click rates increase by up to 300% if a video is included. Videos are easy to record and edit on a smartphone and, whether loaded directly on to LinkedIn or YouTube, they are easy to include in your emails. They will grab the attention of your audience and provide them with easy-to-see, easy-to-listen-to information of value.

- Create compelling subject lines. Who sent the email and the subject line are two main factors in people deciding whether to open the email. The A in AIDA is 'attention'. Your subject header has to grab the attention of the reader, or they may not open your email, even though they know you. Keep in mind that while subject lines should be creative and engaging, they must give your recipient an accurate picture of what to expect when they do open the email. It is the label on the tin. If the label says 'baked beans', then there must be baked beans inside, or you are in trouble.

- The open rate increases by 17% when the subject line is personalised.

- As with the earlier discussion about direct mail:

  - Invest in good images and branding

  - Invest in good copywriting

  - Use the AIDA formula as part of the copywriting

  - Make the reader feel something

  - Include a clear, single call to action

  - Use email in a mix of other methods

  - Make it uncommon

 Building block eight – telemarketing and telesales

Telemarketing, sometimes called telesales or cold calling, definitely does not work anymore. Does it?

In 1967, a PR consultant named Murray Roman launched the first-ever phone-based mass-marketing campaign. Around 15,000 housewives were hired and trained to make about 1 million calls a day on behalf of Ford Motors. The campaign's goal was simply to identify likely automobile buyers – lead generation, rather than trying to sell anything. The campaign is reported to have helped Ford sell 40,000 cars.

For too long, business-to-business (B2B) telemarketing has been considered the poor relation, even the naughty child of the marketing mix. And yet, the average ROI for B2B telemarketing is £11 for every £1 spent. I have personally built all my businesses with telemarketing as a large part of the sales strategy. I know that a few phone calls to the right people, with the right things to say, will win large and profitable business.

B2B and business-to-consumer (B2C) are in some ways remarkably similar. They are both H2H. Human-to-human. Even if we restrict the conversations to marketing and stop ourselves from straying into sales, telemarketing can be used for lead generation. It can turn someone who was not even thinking about x to start considering it. It can be used to nurture leads, turning a "No" to a "Not now" and later to "Tell me more". With an e-shot that original, "No" could mean the email was deleted and the person unsubscribed.

Yet another thing that stands out from the research is how well telemarketing integrates with other channels. Effective marketing has always been better when multichannel. So, telemarketing is not the poor relative. Telemarketing is a worthy fiancé and the ideal marriage partner is email. Email marketing and telemarketing are a marriage made in marketing heaven. With GDPR in place, cold calling from an unchecked list of telephone numbers is not recommended. The Telephone Preference Service does need to be considered. That said, having secured details from an email marketing opt-in, a connection on LinkedIn or even a networking event or exhibition business card swap, you should have enough confidence to pick up the phone on the grounds that you have relevant and meaningful interest. Don't you?

Overleaf are two examples of multichannel or integrated marketing, one for B2B and the other for B2C.

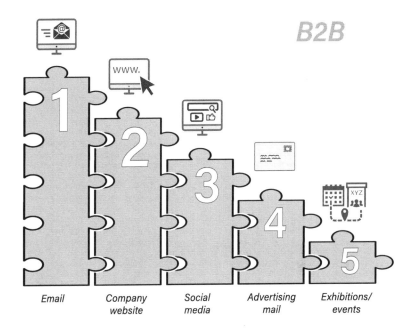

B2B

| Email | Company website | Social media | Advertising mail | Exhibitions/ events |

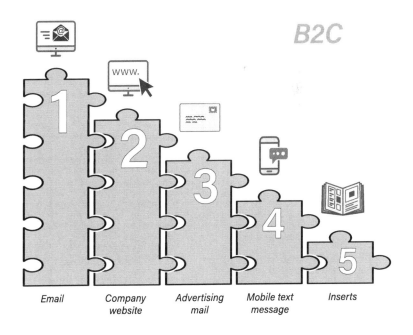

B2C

| Email | Company website | Advertising mail | Mobile text message | Inserts |

Remember these key strategies for your telemarketing or telesales campaign

- Have a small number, I mean no more than three, clear business objectives that will pay you and the business back handsomely.

- It is a good idea to put a lot of time and effort into creating the proposition and call framework or script. Whether it is just you calling – or 15,000 housewives as in the case of Ford Motors – a framework or script that you mostly stick to will ensure scalable and repeatable success.

- Too often, not enough time is put into cleaning data – avoid that mistake. Buy good data and then clean it first; 25% of even good data can be out of date. Clean your own data too – even six months can be a long time in most industries; people change jobs and business start and fail.

- Combine telemarketing with at least one other marketing strategy. Email is the obvious one. Combine three, four, five or all your seven channels if you wish. Integrate offline and online, join up the dots between anything sales and marketing for the biggest return on your investment. And remember to use marketing automation as part of that mix.

- Train your team, or if it is just you, find someone to engage in role-playing with you. Practise with a coach; perfect practice makes perfection permanent, anything else solidifies errors.

- Obey the law, even when if seems to be getting in your way. Your reputation and credibility is more important than any single sale and any single initiative. It forms a vital part of your current and future wealth. It is hard to build and is lost easily, in an instant. Google 'Gerald Ratner jewellery 1992' to see how an entire business can be devalued by one daft comment.

- Use the telephone to book field appointments or to set up video meetings. Such phone calls need be only five to seven minutes long: remember that you are selling only the benefits of an appointment and nothing else.

- Consider sending links by WhatsApp or email to initiate an online demonstration or online seminar.

- Set a goal to move the best leads and enquiries to Zoom, Skype, Google Meet, Webex or GoToMeeting. Video conferencing and one-to-one video calls provide that bit extra – the bridge between telephone and face-to-face meetings. You can see and be seen, which is a massive advantage in many circumstances. And when you have those video meetings, please remember to set your camera at eye level; no one wants to look up your nose. There are plenty of adjustable laptop stands at a reasonable price, so you don't have to spend a fortune on standing desks. Get a good microphone or headset, as a clear audio is a must, then you are set. Conducting proposals via Zoom and even showing videos of product demonstrations or video testimonials work a treat.

If you want the special guide that I've created to help you book as many face-to-face or video meetings as you need, visit www.bemoreeffective.com/theprofitsecret and if you are a first-time visitor, register and download the *Make Appointments by Phone Guide.*

CHAPTER 10

The roof:
your sales
conversation

Like anything in life, prevention is better than cure. With prevention, you have more control over what you do, and when and where you do it. Value protection strategies should start from initial contact with the prospect and continue through every part of every conversation.

Build a Great Roof

By taking this preventive approach, what are you trying to achieve? Much further on in your sales process, you want to be in a position where the prospect is comfortable engaging with your diagnostic questions, listening to your proposals of value and making a decision based on well-balanced criteria rather than just price. You certainly don't want to be in a position where the prospect is voicing concerns such as, "Is that your best price?" or "I've had a cheaper quote." So, your aim from the very start of your process should be to:

- manage aspirations
- engage prospects in authentic diagnosis
- gain insight into the criteria they value
- reduce the probability of the prospect voicing price concerns
- flush out those who seek the lowest price and nothing else

To help do this, you build certain mechanisms into your sales conversations.

What is a mechanism?

Imagine it as something you may do or say at a specific stage of a sales conversation. This could range from a simple statement, a question you ask, an email you may wish to send, right through to something more complex, such the structure of a formal meeting or a detailed proposal.

Among other things, mechanisms can help you slow down, control or redirect a conversation; they help you set or readjust the prospect's expectations and draw out feedback or a commitment.

Setting call objectives

Historically, salespeople were encouraged to set 'call objectives' for each call they made to their prospects or customers. Managers encouraged their salespeople to think about what they were going to do in the meeting, for example:

- Establish the prospects' needs
- Make a presentation on either a specific product or project
- Discuss a new service

These examples all focus on the actions of the salesperson, rather than the prospect. The question you should be asking is:

> "What action do I want my prospect to take as a result of me taking these actions in this meeting?"

- To do this, you need to shift your focus from what you do to what the prospect does. You cannot move the sale forward in any way without the involvement of the prospect. This outcome must be expressed in a way that involves the prospect saying or doing something, for example:
- The prospect agrees on a date for a diagnostic discussion with you
- The prospect agrees with your payback calculation and to recommend your solution to their board

Create a valuable relationship

The very beginning of our first conversation, be it over the phone, by video or face-to-face, is where we set the tone and mood of the dialogue.

Rapport and trust are part of the Profit Secret

A *New York Times* poll is quoted as asking, 'What percentage of people in general are trustworthy?' The answer was apparently 30%. While I cannot find the original poll, for me the answer feels right. What do you think?

Apparently, the newspaper then asked a similar group a slightly different question. 'What percentage of people whom you know are trustworthy?' The answer: 70%. That is a huge difference and again for me feels right. What does it mean? That when people get to know you, and start to like you, people begin to trust you.

What do rapport and trust mean?

Generally, rapport means a harmonious relationship in which the people concerned understand one another's feelings or ideas and communicate well. For me, rapport precedes trust because if you cannot communicate effectively and get on the same page, you are unlikely to develop trust.

The three key elements are:

- **Integrity.** You must be yourself, natural and real. People find it hard to build rapport with a fake front.

- **Competence.** If you do not display a reasonable ability to hold a conversation, building rapport is harder.

- **Compassion.** Showing that you care and are interested in the other person is a key part of building rapport.

Trust can be defined as confidence, faith or belief in someone or something. That is more than being able to communicate well; now I can rely on or believe what you say.

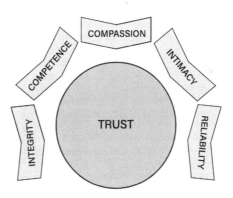

The additional components of trust are:

- **Intimacy.** Trust comes only with a much closer relationship or a deeper understanding.

- **Reliability.** There is a consistent body of evidence that our words and actions can be relied upon. What we say and do add up – repeatedly.

What is the value of rapport and trust?

It is the quality of a relationship that earns you the right to say or ask things. The better the connection, the easier it is to ask difficult questions, disagree or offer advice. Rapport is a mechanism; by developing rapport you earn the right to ask more meaningful questions, which increase your understanding of the other person. As you demonstrate that deeper understanding, you earn the respect of that person so gaining permission to ask even tougher questions.

A LinkedIn survey in the US, reported in *The State of Sales 2018*, confirmed that trust is key to closing deals. While 40% of sales professionals ranked trust as the No. 1 factor in closing deals, above ROI and price; 51% of decision-makers ranked trust as the top factor they desire in a salesperson. Put it this way, as a salesperson, if you cannot be trusted, then nothing that you offer has any value.

How do you build rapport?

Starting a conversation with small talk phrases such as, "How are you?" when you do not know the person tend to be considered a waste of time by the prospect, or even a little insulting. Preliminary pleasantries in video calls or face-to-face meetings are more acceptable. Avoid trite questions and answers. Even "How was lunch?" or "How has the morning been so far?" are both better than "How are you?" In your reply to their question, "How about you?" you could add something unusual, such as, "Yeah, made some progress today – a bit of a challenge though. I am sure you know what I mean?" Being more open and self-revealing chips away at the preconception of salespeople being fake and willing to say anything to get the sale. Everything either helps you or gets in your way.

Humour works. Laughter goes a long way in establishing a personal bond with a prospect. I don't mean telling jokes; they can backfire. Real life is generally funnier especially if the funny story is a self-deprecating one about you.

Compliments work. When directed at something their company or they have produced. It could be as simple as highlighting something about their website, social media posts or products. The key is sincerity. People will sense if you are not being genuine.

Early yeses work. Ask some questions early on specifically designed to get a 'yes' response. Early yeses generally lead to more yeses, partly because of the positive atmosphere they create.

Mirror and matching work. Why? Because people like people who are similar to themselves in some ways. If I apparently unconsciously imitate a gesture, posture, speech pattern, or attitude of my prospect, then I look or sound a little bit like them. Here are three examples:

- **Body language.** If you are facing the prospect and they sit upright with their left elbow on the table, you might sit upright with the right elbow on the table (mirror) or the left (match). Both send a positive subconscious message that you are paying attention to them.

- **Voice.** The easiest two aspects of speech to match are pace and volume. Speak at a similar pace to theirs and at a similar level, without shouting or whispering. Do not mimic accents – that is taken as an insult.

- **Words.** If they call a spade a shovel, call it a shovel. If they use analytical or data-focused style of words and phrases, go with that. If they talk primarily about results, go with that.

Common experiences work. Social media has made it easy for us to research our prospects beforehand and uncover some common or similar experiences. During the conversation, you can then ask a question that brings one or two of those topics up.

Listening works. Listening isn't merely hearing; it is suspending your thoughts so you can understand what a person really means. By genuinely listening to another person you are giving them attention, acceptance and approval. You make them feel important, understood, appreciated and respected. We discussed this at length in Chapter 6. Listening is part of the Profit Secret. Far too many salespeople talk far too much. Telling is not selling.

How do you build trust?

The easiest way to sell at a higher price more often is to make trust central to who you are and everything you do. The higher the degree of trust, the less price will be an issue because with trust there cannot be any manipulation. To be a trusted adviser means that you focus on enabling others to see and achieve what they were not sure they could – your advice helped make something of value happen for them.

You can build rapport by demonstrating that you understand the buyer and by demonstrating that you share values. You can be professional by respecting time, having an agenda and focusing on the prospect's needs and objectives. You build trust by providing value in a conversation, regardless of the outcome, rather than solely using the conversation to position the value of what you sell.

You can build trust by speaking honestly. By doing what you say you will do by the deadline you voluntarily set. By sticking to what you agreed. By admitting if you have made a mistake, by taking ownership rather than blaming others. By speaking only good of others as well as complimenting or thanking others instead of being self-promoting, and by being helpful, by adding value in every conversation and situation that you can.

Building trust starts with two things: being trustworthy and being trusting. You must demonstrate a willingness to trust others. These two are opposite sides of the same coin. And that coin may be one of the most important components of the Profit Secret.

Creating value in the agenda

The opening gambit is a mechanism to put value, in the prospect's terms, at the heart of the reason for talking. It also sets out your expectations in fair and reasonable terms. Here is an example:

> Thank you for your time, Mr Smith. The main purpose of the discussion with you today is to:
>
> - Understand what's important to you in the way you organise x (whatever your product or service helps with)
>
> - Show you how other companies like ABC solved their issue with x
>
> - And to see how we might move things forward at the end. Does that sound reasonable, Mr Smith?
>
>   - Their response: Yes, sure.
>
> - What would you like to get out of our discussion?
>
>   - Their response: The same really.
>
> - How long have you put aside?
>
>   - Their response: About an hour.
>
> - Great, where would you like to start?
>
>   - Their response: I don't mind.

The opening gambit is designed to set the scene, set expectations and seek the first agreements from the prospect, expressed in terms of their self-interest. Even if it is not the first meeting or conversation, if it is the second or fourteenth, you should still set objectives, the buyer's and yours, at the beginning of any meeting. Remember to clarify how much time you have together; the only thing worse than running out of time is running over time.

Developing a strong value proposition

A value proposition is a mechanism used early in conversation to boil down the complexity of your sales pitch into something that your prospect can easily grasp and remember. It is therefore vital that you can articulate this naturally, authentically and enthusiastically.

It is a short collection of reasons why the prospect would benefit from buying something, based on an understanding of their most likely needs. It aims to open your prospect's mind to the idea that one product or service may add more value or better solve a problem than other alternatives. It connects with the ideal customer statement from Chapter 3.

It is not just a statement; it is a whole concept about why people have already bought from you. It describes your uncommon advantage at work. While you should aim for a statement of between 50 and 100 words, you don't want to reduce it so much that there's too little substance left.

A value proposition contains an indication of:

- your uncommon capability or advantage
- your track record
- the problem or pain you solve
- the benefit they can expect

It is phrased in their self-interest (more 'you' than 'I')

It uses persuasive words such as:

- maximise, increase, grow, productivity
- minimise, reduce, decease, eliminate
- fully, completely, now, immediately, rapid
- because, systems and options

The main reasons why people buy fall into three major groupings that, in turn, form the three rules of great value propositions:

1. Potential buyers must need what you are offering.

    The problem or pain you highlight must *resonate* with them.

2. Potential buyers must see how you stand out from the alternatives.

    You must *differentiate*.

3. Potential buyers must believe that you can deliver on your promises.

    You must *substantiate*.

What happens if you do not follow the value proposition rules?

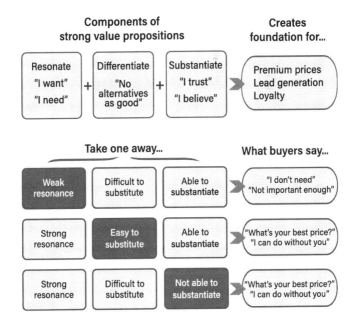

As you can see from the graphic above, break any rule and it makes it much more difficult to sell.

If you want to resonate, differentiate and substantiate, you need to do much more than write a short sentence. Your value proposition, the collection of reasons people buy from you, is woven into the fabric of your organisation and your relationships with current clients. Your track record is then communicated through the collection of statements you make to the market.

Here is one example of a value proposition

I work with business owners who are excited by sustainable growth and want an exceptional sales coaching experience. This is based on 15 years of turning poorly performing sales teams around, for example at Jones Ltd. That involved improving poor conversion ratios, lifting sales turnover and improving team motivation, which led to a reduction in customer acquisition costs. Would you like to explore how you might benefit in a similar way?

In summary, using mechanisms such as establishing rapport, building trust, the opening gambit and the value proposition, alongside good interpersonal skills and a great attitude, go a long way to creating a valuable relationship.

> **If you would like to create a top-notch value proposition, visit www.bemoreeffective.com/theprofitsecrets and if you are a first-time visitor, register and download the *Value Proposition Worksheet.***

Understand what is valuable to the prospect

This requires the development of precise, targeted questions and great listening skills. Asking questions is regarded as one of the most important mechanisms. Asking great questions is part of the Profit Secret.

Not just any questions asked in a robotic, question-and-answer interrogation style. You want to ask questions on a bed of rapport and trust, so your questions are part of your insatiable, humble curiosity, rather than being obtrusive or critical. Through your questions, you show that you are interested and want to understand. Why is this important?

"I don't care how much you know until I know how much you care."

Only once the prospect believes that you want to understand what's important to them and that you care, they are more receptive to your deeper questioning now and the ideas or solutions you put forward later.

Until value is established, any price is too high

The best style of questioning is consultative. The Oxford English Dictionary defines the word 'consultant' as '*a person who provides expert advice professionally*'. And although you know that your whole approach in terms of your style, mannerisms, actions and behaviours should be in line with that of a consultant, the key lies in your problem diagnostic capabilities ahead of your problem-solving ones.

You've heard the saying, in relation to medical doctors, 'Prescription before diagnosis is malpractice'. Well, this is true in business and sales too, hence the investigation stage (questioning) of the sales process being the most important. That is where value is defined. The value is found in the pain of the present, and therefore, the sale is made in the diagnostic stage. That is where the evidence exists for the need for change: the ROI generated by changing and the cost of not changing. The fact that the sale is made in the pain of the present and not in the benefits of the bright future you will later offer is part of the Profit Secret.

Developing your targeted questions

Clearly, it is far better for you to develop your own guided questions than learn something by rote from others. Through the insights and examples below, you can develop your own set of questions that are relevant for your company and the type of prospects to whom you sell.

Remember to ask for observations rather than opinions. The easiest way to do this is to avoid asking 'why' questions. Opinions differ between people in a decision-making unit and can make selling harder. Facts and evidence make for a stronger business case. This is another part of the Profit Secret.

Current situation

Initially your questions should be orienting, seeking out a platform of information from which you can home in on certain key areas. A little like taking a photograph in that it is a snapshot image of the present.

- "How do you organise things at the moment?" Notice this is very general, not specific. It is designed deliberately to get the customer talking.

- How many offices? How many people? What products do you manufacture? (data-finding questions).

You want to get them talking. The more they talk, the better they feel. Everyone's attention level is higher when talking, so they feel better. The more they talk, the more they trust us, if we are listening well. Start with mainly positive questions to get some dopamine (the happiness drug) flowing in the brain. Mix these with the data-finding questions and you will be amazed by how many extra snippets of information come out that you can refer to later.

Discovery questions

Questions that uncover problems and needs can help the prospect sense the value we could bring. Our questions highlight an area that could be improved. They highlight the consequences of that pain and the likely damage caused by doing nothing. While value does not have to be financial, it does have to be meaningful. And remember that the absence of meaningful value is as much of a pain as a costly problem. That is part of the Profit Secret.

Individual needs

What is influencing the individual or individuals who will decide to engage your services? These needs are often unspoken and less obviously connected to your services. While you cannot always uncover these types of needs directly, by being aware of what may be going on you can be alert to the obstacles that could keep you from connecting your services with your prospect's needs. They include professional, social and psychological needs.

Organisational needs

What is their business trying to accomplish or avoid? What problems are they trying to solve? What opportunities would they like to exploit?

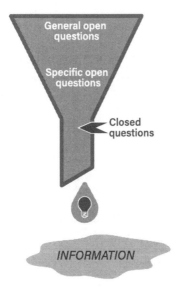

These can be categorised as:

- **Strategic.** The need to expand into a new market. The need to stop top talent leaving. The need to increase profit, revenue, and share price.

  They don't need a marketing plan, HR plan or sales training programme.

- **Technical.** The need to stop IT servers going down so often. The need to reduce picking and shipping errors. The need to reduce time to market for new products.

  They don't need a new monitoring service, a quality study or process reengineering consultant.

- **Financial.** The need to reduce overheads. The need to improve cashflow. The need to reduce the cost of customer acquisition.

  Not a cost-reduction analysis. Not a new invoice factoring service. Not a value stream mapping study.

- **Political or environmental.** The need to cut expenditure on single-use plastic. The need to allow a new store to be built. The need to avoid bad publicity.

  Not a new packaging design, a grassroots campaign or series of press releases.

Value can be realised in many ways, for example, to:

- solve a business or personal problem
- improve a business process
- create a business opportunity
- realise a business objective
- reduce a business risk
- reduce or eliminate business cost

Value can be classified in terms of the four Es:

- **Economies.** Help them save money
- **Efficiencies.** Help them save time, materials, and effort

- **Effectiveness**. Help them produce better results
- **Edge**. Help give them a competitive edge in their market

More desire equals less resistance

The more areas you probe through tactical questioning, and the more opportunities you find now to add value, the less likely resistance will appear with any degree of strength later. Certainly, you know from personal experience that the more you desire something, the less you can resist it. Think about going out shopping for clothes. You may look at a shirt, suit, dress, shoes etc and know that you cannot afford it. "Do I really need it?" you may ask yourself. "Haven't I got enough shirts?"

Yet as you continue to look at the piece of clothing in the shop window and imagine how you might use it, the more you desire it, until at some point you buy it because you cannot resist. The principle is the same with prospects and you want to create and build value in the mind of your prospect so that resistance becomes weaker. That is part of the Profit Secret.

Tactical probing

To get the right type of information, you need to ask the right type of questions.

When asking questions, it is far better to uncover and establish value in the mind of the prospect by asking questions relating to the areas and topics that are important to them. The concept of value is always defined in the prospect's terms.

The concept of value is subjective and people define it differently, so for your value to be irresistible in your prospect's eyes, you should always seek to find those terms of definition from their point of view. The value house sales approach will always uncover a different concept of value for every prospect; everyone's needs and requirements are unique. And that is a vital part of the Profit Secret – uncover and deliver different, relevant and meaningful value to each client.

Once you can get a prospect to define value in their terms, you are then in a good position to offer your proposals using those same terms. This will be very attractive to them as the proposal describes what they value in their own words.

The information you need will include:

- the evidence for their needs and wants
- their thoughts, concerns and motivations, in their words
- how they define value
- what is important to them
- what results they want
- what success will look like to them
- how they will measure success
- what they want to avoid
- the evidence for the symptoms, problems and root causes they want to remove

People do not buy from salespeople because they understand their products, but because they felt that the salesperson understood their problems. That is part of the Profit Secret.

Asking precise, diagnostic and value-based questions is a crucial part of the Profit Secret. It is impossible to consistently sell more at a higher margin unless you ask the right type of questions, in the right areas, to find the right information. It is the information you gain from the prospect that is translated into value for the prospect, who becomes your customer.

Widen the gap by asking about frequency and impact:

- How often does this happen?
- What effect does it have on other parts of the business?
- What does this cost in time, effort, lost production, financially?
- What are the implications or costs of doing nothing?

Use questions that highlight problems, build desire and create urgency:

- What are you missing out on because of the slow turnaround?
- How else would you benefit from achieving a 24-hour turnaround?
- How would that help you? Help others?
- What other problems is the slow turnaround causing?
- What else would change for the better if you could create greater output while achieving greater control?
- What have these issues cost you in the past 12 months?
- Of the things you've mentioned so far, which is the most important?
- What makes that one more important than the rest?
- When do you need to start seeing these benefits being delivered through improved key performance measures on your side?
- What makes that timeframe important?

These are just the start, because from there you can develop more tactical questions that encourage and facilitate the prospect telling you what else is important and how much of a priority those other criteria are.

Follow the pain chain

Pain chains are diagrams or words that identify the key players and their pains. They describe contributing reasons for their problems, and the knock-on impacts of those pains on others in the organisation. They capture the interdependence across several decision-makers and influencers and help you identify a more complete scale and cost of the problem, and make a stronger business case for change.

Your polite, humble and insatiable curiosity will enable you to secure internal referrals as you willingly seek evidence to test a hypothesis on your original prospect's behalf – and you'll probably do much of this for free because this mechanism is part of the Profit Secret and enables you to uncover exactly what you can sell at a higher value more often.

Preventive questions

The following questions seek to establish the relative importance to the prospect of different decision-making criteria that you suspect to be a common factor in your target market. Select those that suit you the best, or even better, use these examples as a springboard to come up with your own:

- Other than price, what is important to you?

- What are some of the things you look for in a supplier?

- How do you reconcile quality against cost?

- How do we demonstrate the credibility required to do business with you?

- What would you and I need to discuss and agree on for you to feel 100% comfortable doing business with us?

- How important is control and flexibility to you on this project?

- Mr Prospect, our clients speak very highly of the quality of our work; in fact, some say they choose us even though they initially considered us one of the more expensive providers. Is a high price going to be a problem for you?

- Inevitably, we will need to talk about the cost of this solution. It may be useful therefore to take a couple of minutes now to understand what your expectations of the total cost will be. Are you thinking £40k, £30k or £20k? (use round numbers, the highest number first).

- Inevitably, you will need to justify this investment to your colleagues. It may be useful to explore what ROI or payback period has previously been accepted on capital expenditure purchases. What is the norm? A four-year payback? Three years? Two years?

If you would like help to challenge and to improve the questions you ask your prospects, visit www.bemoreeffective.com/ theprofitsecret and if you are a first-time visitor, register and download the *Value Discovery Question Worksheet*.

Signposts

Signposts are mechanisms that allow you to slow the conversation down and encourage the prospect to listen to questions and to give you high-quality information in their answers, or a statement that gets you a heightened level of attention. Examples of this are:

- May I ask you a different type of question?

- Later, I will share another factor that many say is significant.

- I will tell you more about x later.

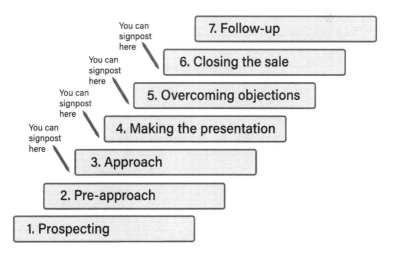

Signposts generate attention. When using a signpost as a question, it helps ensure the question does not get lost in the 'ether'.

Signposts improve the flow of precious information. They serve you in a positive way because they help you in your quest to sell more at a higher price. You can signpost anywhere in the process. Signposting is an essential tool in ensuring that your communication is seamless, effortless and enjoyable for the prospect.

Summarising

Summarising allows you to 'play back' your understanding of what you have heard or has just been agreed between the two of you. It allows you to state again the facts relating to criteria that they said were important. Summarising avoids misunderstanding.

"It is better to understand a little than to misunderstand a lot."

– Anatole France

The more you can ensure that the information that has been shared is agreed and understood, the better. The more that the essential elements are repeated and confirmed openly, the more validity your proposal will have when it is based on this information. Especially when that proposal has their voice and their choice of words all over it.

Getting feedback

Did you know all good salespeople are heat-seeking missiles?

Imagine you can see a heat-seeking missile. It is called a heat-seeking missile because it relies totally on the heat from its target to guide it in. Well in a way, salespeople, your questions and your presentations are heat-seeking missiles. The prospect's feedback allows you to see where you are and whether you need to adjust the direction of your questioning, the relevance of the solution you put forward or the type of commitment you seek. Listening to and adjusting to the feedback helps you avoid any potential mismatch in terms of expectations later when it is much more difficult to handle.

How often should you seek feedback from the prospect? All the time! Feedback is part of the Profit Secret.

How do you get feedback? Sprinkle your conversations with evaluative questions when you discover something of value to the prospect. It may sound something along the lines of:

- "Does that make sense?"
- "So quality is key to you then?"
- "So, although price is important, you wouldn't sacrifice quality and service to get something cheap; have I got that right?"

Getting feedback is crucial as it is another mechanism that allows you to confirm you are on a sound footing; that the factors and criteria you are using to demonstrate added value in your proposal are the right ones.

Propose what is valuable to them

Someone once said that a focused sales presentation is a little like those round magnets that either attract or repel other metal objects, including other magnets. Imagine you have a magnet in your hand that attracts other magnets. We've all done it, I'm sure, where we put our magnet close to these other magnets and they immediately get 'sucked up' and locked on to the magnet we hold in our hand.

Imagine then that the magnet you hold in your hand is one that represents your prospect's expressed and confirmed needs, and that it attracts only the specific points of value that your company can deliver in the different and uncommon way your prospect is excited by. Anything about your company or your capability that does *not* relate to the prospect's needs are the opposing magnets; even when you try to put them together, they simply force themselves apart.

What is value?

Value is whatever the prospect thinks is valuable. If you assume you know what the prospect wants without asking them, you will be wrong.

Saving time may be valuable, and if that's the case, your proposal needs to focus on how you will meet or beat schedule deadlines, solving their problem of lost productivity while still giving the prospect the other services they want.

The proposal you subsequently present, in whatever format, should focus on demonstrating the benefits of what you offer, matched and dovetailed specifically with the needs and wants voiced by the prospect in the questioning phase. And nothing else.

When deciding which of your company's selling points to include and which to leave out, exclude those with no relevance. Prioritise those you do include in line with what is critical to the prospect, with the aim of demonstrating through your proposal that in those important areas for them, that is where you are the strongest. It is not always possible to create an exact match so get as close as you can, as in the diagram above. Ensure your proposition contains these three elements.

- **Essential.** There will be some aspects of your product or service that are the attractive magnets for this prospect to hear because they have a direct correlation and impact on their need and they match their aspirations.

- **Desirable.** These are aspects of your product or service that are not necessarily essential. It would be useful for the prospect to consider them and their potential impact and benefit. As you often sell more by offering fewer options, avoid the temptation to include too many desirable items that don't match a specific expressed need.

- **Game changer.** This is an uncommon answer to a blend of needs that you have creatively put together. While your prospect did express each need separately, they did not consider the connection in the way you have. Your competition would not have thought of this solution. It is a major differentiator adding significant value and as such is part of the Profit Secret.

Good, better, best

One part of the Profit Secret hidden in plain sight is tiered pricing. There is nothing new about adding or subtracting product features to create variably priced bundles targeted at prospects of varying economic means or those who value features differently. Back in the 1930s, Alfred P Sloan introduced a price ladder to differentiate Chevrolets and Buicks from Oldsmobiles and Cadillacs, thus enabling General Motors to overtake Ford by creating 'a car for every purse and purpose'.

In 2018, a *Harvard Business Review* article recommended that companies should pay close attention to the price gaps between 'good', 'better' and 'best'. Its advice was that a 'good' price should be no less than 25% below 'better', and a 'best' price no more than 50% above 'better'. Between 30% and 60% of your revenue could come from buyers opting for the 'best'. Yet many salespeople and companies have not yet adopted tiered pricing. One Profit Secret is to offer different value to each different prospect with three alternatives: 'good', 'better' and 'best'.

A presentation structure you could consider is:

Start with a demonstration to the prospect that you understand their needs. Use their voice and the voices of other stakeholders. This will continue to build your credibility and motivate them more to listen to your proposals. This understanding should include:

- What the current situation is – what they do and what is currently happening

- Some of the issues, challenges and pain points they experience

- The cost to their business now and the cost of doing nothing

- The objective they would like to achieve, the results they want and what 'good looks like'

- An agreement from the prospect that your understanding is correct and that they would like to find a solution to address these problems or issues

Continue with an overview of the solution you are going to present, offering some carrots up front and the key results you will achieve, followed by:

- Taking one agreed issue at a time

- Connecting each essential selling point to the issue

- Continuing to translate that selling point into a compelling benefit by explaining how the application solves the different problems in the pain chain, ideally in their choice of words, their voice

- Describing the positive future benefits that they will enjoy beyond the decision to buy

- Asking for feedback with evaluative questions, such as "How does that sound?"

- Introducing the second essential selling point and repeating the process above

- Introducing the third essential selling point, as above

Stop at three selling points. Start and finish strong; put your weakest selling point in the middle.

Finish with a concise summary of the key points:

- Making sure you highlight the key issue they face coupled with the solution you offer in one sentence – a version of the win statement we will discuss shortly

- Keeping the summary points to no more than three anchors, as they are more likely to remember them – less is more.

There should be a lot of overt and explicit links between the needs and issues identified with the prospect, and how selected benefits of your product or service connect to those issues. This 'connective tissue' is how you show and tell them that what you do connects explicitly to their needs. To help highlight the connective statement, use phrases such as:

- "Which means that..."
- "How this will help you is..."
- "I mentioned this because I know you'd like to..."
- "The way this will affect output is..."

These mechanisms help ensure that you are hitting their 'sweet spot' in a compelling way.

Calculating benefits to help create buyer value

Your proposal needs to measure precisely how your product or service will make or save money for each buyer – the financial benefits. This provides compelling financial reasons to make a change. Wherever possible, show the ROI calculation or the estimated payback period.

Showing non-financial benefits to help create buyer value

There are benefits that are not so easily measured in monetary terms; things such as 'operational excellence' or 'product leadership'.

Most are still quantifiable and measurable, and while we all buy emotionally, we prefer it when there is sound logic to back up our feelings. We are back to our three Greek friends again: ethos (ethical appeals), pathos (emotional appeals), and logos (logical appeals).

The greater the importance of your product or service to the prospect and the more difficult it would be to substitute what you offer with that of a competitor, the greater the risk for the buyer. Buyers do not like risk. If it is less risky to stay as they are than accept your proposal, they may choose to do nothing. There is pain and cost in change, whether that is changing supplier or changing current practices. Your solution must overcome the friction and inertia caused by change and risk. You must demonstrate that yours is the best solution and the safest – better and safer than doing nothing. That is part of the Profit Secret.

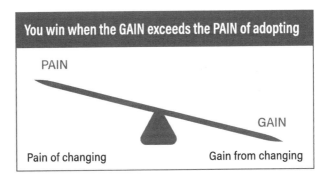

Wherever savings of any kind can be made, be sure to identify, highlight and maximise what they are and how they may impact on the client. By doing this, you are building a stack of value. More desire, less resistance and more ways to defend your price if required.

Win statement

This is a short statement that articulates your total value to the client – one that is punchy, memorable and fact-filled.

To develop your win statement first, take their answers to all your discovery questions, the hard and soft data you used to create your total solution, as well as your solution itself. Put all this into a mental 'winepress' and squeeze out the rest of this statement in 50 words or so.

- We will win this bid if the decision-makers believe…

As far as possible, this should include numbers and be tied directly to the client's bottom line, for example:

> "Based on your assessment that improved information systems of this type will improve output by 10%, this system will pay back £1.9m in the first year and £34.5m over the next five years."

The value in your win statement needs to dwarf your fee so that the ROI and payback period make your price a non-issue.

If you cannot make a value case, then any buyer is right to ask, "Is this worth it?" and "How are we going to pay for this?" With a strong win statement, you are more likely to win the sale. Great win statements are part of the Profit Secret.

Different roles mean different value

Remember that your prospect's role will affect their view of value. Perspective changes everything. A chief executive pays most attention to shareholder value, innovation and competitiveness. An IT director has a split focus between what the technology can deliver to the business operation and the advanced nature of the technology itself. The finance director is more interested in costs, risk and share value. The sales director is focused on competitor differentiation, increasing market share and customer acquisition.

Find the link between each role's perspective and your proposal. This is a great way to demonstrate the vital and viral nature of the value you bring. Each decision-maker would be influenced by a win statement customised for their role.

Summary

All the practical ideas and mechanisms covered in this chapter are designed to give your proposition strength and rigidity. Each element individually offers powerful benefits for your sales approach. When used together, their collective strength offers unparalleled margin-enhancing and protection capability.

However, we realise that in the real world nothing is perfect, and things aren't that black and white. So, in the next chapter we will consider how we can positively manage situations when things do go wrong, situations which we will call 'snagging'.

If you would like to create more persuasive sales presentations and win statements, visit www.bemoreeffective.com/theprofitsecret and if you are a first-time visitor, register and download the *Sales Presentation Guide*.

CHAPTER 11

Resolve snags to keep more of the profit

Resolve concerns

Could anything go wrong when building a house? Of course it could. Building your value house sales model is no different, so in this chapter we will examine how you can ensure that you smooth things out along the way to minimise the risk of too much snagging at the end.

Highlighting the objection before they do

This is an interesting and highly successful mechanism. If you suspect the prospect may raise an objection later in the process, the principle of getting to it before they do generally makes its use by them invalid.

From the very start of your interaction with the prospect, you are a bit like a heat-seeking missile. Without the heat, it is an aimless weapon. As a professional salesperson, you rely on heat; that 'heat' being feedback from the prospect. You may sense their concerns in something that they:

- say or don't say
- do or don't do

Nearly all concerns that come towards the end of the sales process could have been dealt with earlier, leaving the process snag-free.

Penultimate questions

If you do not get any snags voluntarily as you move through the sales process, it is still essential to intentionally ask for them, so you are sure there are none hidden. Use evaluative questions, the penultimate closing mechanism, also known as a trial close, for example:

- "How does that sound to you?"
- "What are your thoughts so far?"
- "Does that make sense?"

To flush out snags, you ask evaluative, feedback-seeking questions as you go. Sprinkle them liberally throughout the interaction. Look and listen out for things such as the prospect:

- saying "Mmmm…" in response to one of your feedback questions
- starting to avoid eye contact or being distracted
- giving vague answers

While there are plenty more, these give you the idea. Of course, the prospect could be more overt with their concerns, for example:

- "I'm not so sure"
- "Sounds expensive"
- Shaking their head.
- Putting your proposal down on the table, closing it and pushing it away.

You should be interpreting constantly what you see or hear from the prospect, asking yourself, "What does that mean?" If unsure, ask an evaluative question. With snagging, you are trying to ensure that the prospect voices their concern so you can understand it and offer a solution straight away. You want to be as sure as you can that when you have finished building your proposition with the value house sales model it is snag-free, before you attempt to close the sale.

If, for example, you suspect they may later say, "It's too expensive," you would bring that into the conversation before offering any proposals or indeed any price. For example:

> "Clearly, I don't want you thinking we are too expensive after we have submitted our proposal. What would you like to see in the proposal to avoid that?"

By discussing this now, it makes it difficult for the prospect to voice that objection later.

If an objection comes

If you get hit by a storm in a real house, you need to be sure the house can withstand the full onslaught of the stormy weather. Any proposition built with the value house sales approach needs to be similarly robust.

If the prospect does raise an objection, despite everything, how best can you respond to it?

The most likely time for objections to be raised is after a proposal has been delivered and you invite feedback from the prospect as part of a trial close.

The mechanism required now is a curative strategy, rather than the preventive approach. The best sales process will *always* include preventive mechanisms much earlier to help eliminate or reduce resistance and objections. Your approach to handling any objection is the same in terms of the process and psychology, except that the words that make up the questions and answers are different. So, let's consider some general principles that apply to any type of objection you could get. Here are some different reactions and the appropriate counter actions.

Reaction   Counter

Disbelief

- Provide some examples
- Prove it
- Use references to convince

Disinterest

- Withdraw – do more research
- Explore disinterest
- Clarify needs further

Dislike

- Clarify
- Revise changeable features
- Show that benefits outweigh drawbacks
- Change sales strategy

Objection handling processes

Here are two of the best mechanisms for answering objections:

1. **Welcome, agree, respond**
2. **Listen, clarify, answer**

   Expanding on No. 2 – this means:

   - Listen first – hear them out fully and emphasise
   - Clarify
     - Ask questions such as, "What more can you tell me?" Probe for a deeper meaning, for the evidence not just the opinion

- Check that it is not a condition – something that is fixed and unmovable
- Isolate the true objection; this is rarely the first issue raised
- Restate the objection in question form
- Answer – use the feel, felt, found method with a written customer testimonial, or preferably a video

Building rapport at all stages

When the pressure is on and things may get tricky, it is important that you aim to build rapport, strengthen trust and stay honest. Indeed, it is these links between you and the prospect that will see you through any challenge. You want to be hard on the issue and soft on the relationship, not the other way around.

- **Hard on the issue** means I have a right to stand my ground, to defend my price and show that it is outstanding value. I will not give in easily, if at all.
- **Soft on the relationship** means that I will continue to be warm, friendly, respectful, professional, consultative and honest with you. I will not fall out with you.

Make sure that you constantly 'thread' throughout the conversation phrases such as:

- "I am very keen to work with you…"
- "I believe we can add real value…"
- "I want to find a way through this…"

Listening and clarifying

Listen to the objection. Resist the temptation to butt in or to answer it. Sometimes just by listening to the prospect talk, they answer their own point.

Then seek to clarify it further by asking additional questions, so that you fully understand their point. Very often when objections are first voiced, they are expressed as the 'skin of the apple'. The real objection is the core. To get to the core, you must take a bite out of the apple. For example, "Price too high" could mean any of the following:

- "I have no money."
- "It is more expensive than I thought it would be or can sanction."
- "I am not convinced of the value."
- "As a professional buyer, I ask every salesperson that."

You must establish the real objection before you can attempt to overcome it.

You do this by empathising first, "Thank you for mentioning that," then clarifying it:

- "Just to clarify my thinking, what makes that important to you?"
- "How do you mean?"
- "I'm sure you have a very good reason for saying that. Do you mind if I ask you what that is?"

Asking questions and listening well also helps re-establish rapport and trust. The positive dynamic of the relationship will have been disturbed by the prospect raising the objection. Inviting them to talk and demonstrating your intention to understand by great listening will go a long way towards re-establishing trust.

Agreement

Once they have explained some of their thinking and feelings, even though you may not agree with the objection itself, you can express your agreement with the logic, intent or thought process behind it. Agreeing serves three main purposes:

1. It softens the objection in the prospect's mind.

2. It offers an alternative to a confrontation.

3. It continues the rebuilding of rapport and trust between you.

Examples

- "I do understand how you feel."

- "That's a good point. I'm glad you brought it up."

- "Another client had a similar reaction initially."

Isolating the true objection

The first issue raised is rarely the real concern bothering them. It is more likely to be one that is easier to mention for some reason. Ask, "Apart from that, what else might cause you to hesitate?" or "Apart from that, what else is on your mind?"

Restating the objection in question form

If the prospect said, "It's a bit expensive," you may say, "So, am I right in thinking that the question is, Mr Smith, could you buy this new system for any less?" or "I guess the question you are asking is: do the extra features that you've selected warrant the price?"

You are seeking confirmation that you understand them, so stick close to what you think the real objection is. You are not trying to redirect them.

The feel, felt, found method

The great thing about this method for overcoming objections is that it demonstrates a high degree of empathy and demonstrates customer benefits through the social proof of others.

- "I understand how you **feel** Peter. If I were in your position, I'd probably feel the same."

- "In fact, some customers we now work with in Manchester initially **felt** pretty much the way you do."

- "Interestingly, after they had spoken to a few clients in similar circumstances, they **found** that those clients had enjoyed even greater returns than I'd stated."

Try this as an exercise

- Write out the three objections you hear most often and then develop a 'feel, felt, found' (FFF) answer for each using a different mini case study.

- Now work out replacement phrases for the FFF ones, such as, "I **see** what you mean," for "I understand how you **feel**," so you can mix up the language to make things sound more natural and less 'salesy'.

- Even better, ask some clients, who as prospects had one of those three objections, to record a one- or two-minute video on their smartphone. They can explain how their experience as clients answers or outweighs that concern. Video testimonials are part of the Profit Secret.

Once you have answered their objection, ask an evaluative question to ensure they believe you have as well, something like, "Are you OK with that?" If they say, "Yes," you are back on the road to agreement.

Gain commitment to action

One part of the Profit Secret is to focus on opening minds rather than closing sales. You earn the right to ask for the business by creating a valuable relationship, establishing what is of unique value to your prospect and presenting that value in a compelling, clear, need-matching way. Now, you can ask for their commitment.

What is closing?

How about making a fair and reasonable request of another person at a fair and reasonable time?

With that definition of 'closing', it does not seem so 'salesy' or challenging. In fact you, me, all of us make requests like that throughout a normal day without batting an eyelid.

- Request: "Could you open the door for me please? I've got my hands full."

  Answer: "Yes." Result! You have just convinced someone to do something. You made a sale!

- Request: "If you can sense some value and common ground today, it would make sense to agree the next step at the end of this meeting. Does that sound fair to you?"

  Answer: "Yes." (It looks as though you've just made another sale!)

Every time you make a fair and reasonable request at a fair and reasonable time, you are closing a sale. We do that all day long, most days, without a problem. Then we find ourselves in something labelled as a selling situation and that easy, natural ability, which we all clearly have, goes straight out of the window.

When should you make a reasonable request?

When should you attempt to close a sale? All the time?

Remember it is the prospect who judges whether the request and the timing is reasonable. Learn to dance with prospects; lead a little, while staying in step. Even from the beginning, on the phone, making the appointment in the first place. Then keep making fair and reasonable requests all the way through the sales conversation. As you can see in the image, a well-timed closing question can be asked as we move from stage to stage in the sales process. This builds a staircase of agreement in the mind of the prospect.

Ultimate closing questions

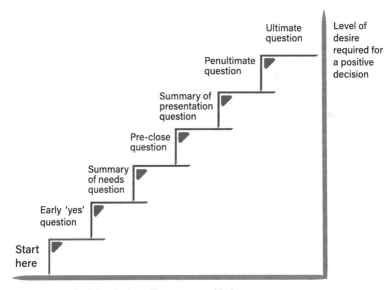

Length of time in the selling process with the prospect

While there are hundreds of complex variations of closing questions, I recommend sticking to the simple ones.

Here are some examples of great closing questions:

Direct

- "May I have your order?"
- "Are you ready to move forward to the next step?"

Assumptive

This is usually not even a question. You need to be convinced that the prospect is keen to go ahead, or you could be perceived to be pushy. Examples include:

- "Send me confirmation by email and I'll get the paperwork ready now."
- "Unless you have any more questions, I think we're ready to get started."

Secondary

Here you ask a question about a secondary decision associated with the big one, the unspoken primary question being, "Will you buy?" Yes or no. If the prospect gives a positive answer to the secondary question, they are ready to buy. Examples include:

- "What delivery date would you like?"
- "Which packaging would you prefer?"

Alternative

Offer them two choices; if the prospect selects one, the deal is done. We all prefer a choice.

- "Which option do you prefer, the blue or the red?"

- "Would you prefer the meeting on Monday morning or Tuesday afternoon?"

If... would...

- "If I were to send over a contract today, would you feel confident signing?"

- "If we could find a way to deal with [objection], would you be willing to sign the contract?"

Soft

- "Mr Prospect, I want you to feel 100% confident before going ahead. What else do you and I have to agree on before you would feel 100% comfortable taking the next step?" If they answer "Nothing," it means the sale is yours.

- "Mr Prospect, what do you consider a fair and reasonable next step?"

Having looked at snagging, we have nearly completed our journey through the value house sales model. But what if the house were exposed to stormy weather during the final stages of the build? What mechanisms do you have to hand that will help repel such difficult conditions? Next, we will look at some key strategies that can help keep the serious stormy weather out.

Price pressure strategies

Having looked at mechanisms that apply to resolving any concerns, we are going to look specifically at the price objection – the nemesis of average salespeople and a banana skin for the best. Dealing with the price objection effectively is part of the Profit Secret. The best mechanism includes four strategies:

1. Defend and justify

2. Negotiate

3. Concede

4. Walk away

Whatever the prospect says to put price pressure on you, there are only four ways a salesperson can respond to price pressure. We will review each of the four strategies in turn and consider the merits and pitfalls of each one as we go. A professional salesperson would use these mechanisms in the order above. In other words, no matter what the question from the prospect is, you will always attempt vigorously to apply strategy one first, the others in turn and the fourth strategy being your last and least preferred strategy.

In the next chapter we will cover defending and justifying the price.

CHAPTER 12

Keeping bad weather out: part one

Strategy one – defend and justify your price

Defend and justify is strategy one for a reason. It is better to think of it as the only position to adopt, rather than, "I'll try to defend the price but if I get more pressure I can always move." Think that and you have already moved. While strategy two is there as a fallback, your focus needs to be 100% on offering sound, mutually beneficial commercial reasons to stick with the current price.

As the saying goes, 'As you go through life, make this your goal: keep your eye on the doughnut and not on the hole'. I think the author was talking about focusing on what you have, not what you do not have.

Most buyers may feel that they are finding your Achilles heel by pushing for a better price. Given the number of average salespeople who give in very quickly to the slightest pressure on price, they may be right. Our discussions about attitudes earlier suggested that if you believed the prospect would get up and walk away if you defended your price, it was your mindset, not your objection handling skills, that needed the work.

If you have good product knowledge, if you fully understand your prospect's needs and believe passionately that you can offer a real value-added solution, defending and justifying your price is the smartest and most commercial position to adopt.

Assuming the prospect asks, "Is this your best price?"

How do we deal with it? One answer could be, "Yes, that is our best price, considering that the benefits outlined match your specific requirements and the payback period is only two years. Why do you ask?"

They may also say, "It's not as good as some other quotes we've had" or "You'll have to do better than that."

You may be tempted to ask, "Better than what?" There are several other things that you could choose to say at that point, depending very much on the relationship and rapport you have.

In terms of being able to defend your price to justify the value, it is worth thinking through how best to respond verbally to certain people and in certain scenarios. The best way is with questions, to seek understanding, to rebuild rapport and to isolate the most important concerns.

Clearly it is best that you work through the ideas in this book, assemble your thoughts and develop your own style to suit your prospects. My aim is to support your learning by sharing with you some ideas that have helped others.

The mechanisms below are representative of some of the best I have come across. While none of them work all the time, they do all work. The most successful salespeople I know are the ones who have the widest choice of mechanisms available to them and know which one is best for the different situations they find themselves in.

Some great questions you might ask

> "Putting price aside, which other aspects of our package are you unhappy with?"

Try to 'isolate' the objection. Determine whether there are any other concerns the prospect may have hidden. If they say, "None," this shows that they are very happy with everything else you have proposed and there is a high degree of buying desire. All that remains is the price versus value discussion.

If they say there are other issues, then price is not the only one. It may not even be a significant issue, despite it being offered up as the first line of resistance. What you must do is ask, "What are the other issues?" so you can understand which issue you do need to deal with. It is likely that by solving one of the other concerns they have you can reduce or eliminate the feeling that you are too expensive. Isolating the true objection is always a sound approach.

If you do not isolate the true objection, it is possible that as you attempt to answer the initial objection, a second will be put forward. This second concern may or may not be connected to their first point. You answered the first point believing that by answering you would be back on the road to agreement. Confronted by a series of objections, feelings of frustration could set in on both sides.

> "Before I respond to that, let me ask you, if you could create a product that was perfect for you, that matched your every need, how close do you think it would compare to mine?"

This mechanism is designed to encourage the prospect to identify how close your proposition is to their ideal. Often, by talking aloud they find that it is not that far off. By them verbalising how close your proposition is to their ideal, they also build their own desire for it. Remember, the more buying desire, the less resistance. And this question also moves their thoughts away from price and focuses them on value. Always a good idea.

> "What are you comparing the price to?"

Is there another proposal under consideration? By drawing out from the prospect that there is a 'something else' you have a chance. Identifying that 'something' means you can discuss the benchmarking exercise that is going on in their head and offer alternative perspectives on the best answer. If the 'something' is budget, you can discuss payment term periods or budget allocation. If it is a competitor, you can discuss whether it is 'like for like'. Remember the SWOT analysis and uncommon advantage statement from earlier? Use these mechanisms to prove that your offering *isn't* the same and there *are* valuable differences.

Of course, your question could draw out that they are not comparing your proposal to anything. It is merely a knee-jerk reaction – by suggesting a logical approach, you can reveal and disarm their subjective thinking.

> "Let me ask you, do you tend to buy based on price or value?"

To use this mechanism, you need a solid relationship as well as the right tone of voice to ensure that your question is not perceived as offensive.

The answer to this question is normally, "Value," followed rapidly by, "Well, both actually." This allows you to follow up with another question, "I appreciate that, Mr Prospect, how do you reconcile costs against value?" Remember, you are defending and justifying your price, so aim to steer the discussion on to the topic of value, where you almost always have more influence.

> "So is money the only concern?"

Trying to isolate the objection again. The prospect may say, "Well, no, it's not my only concern – but it is a concern." Great news, there is something else to discuss other than price, so you ask, "OK, I understand that, Mr Prospect. A project like this has many complexities for you to consider. For me to help you best and ensure the maximum value can be achieved for you, may I ask you…?" Notice you didn't mention price or dropping your price.

Now you discuss their concerns other than price. Embrace as many of their concerns as possible because then it is highly unlikely that you will be faced with that original issue, price, again.

> "Just so I understand, are you saying that it is too expensive, or that the returns it will give you seem insufficient?"

This response is clearly encouraging the prospect to clarify whether the returns generated by the solution *are* or *are not* great enough.

If they say the returns are *not* sufficient, then any price will be too high. The easiest way for someone to react if they feel they are not getting sufficient value is to use the price as the reason. The first objection used often sounds like a good excuse to the prospect.

The challenge now is to ensure the discussion that follows focuses on the returns they will get, as well as the benefits matching the needs they have identified. There could be a misunderstanding as to what constitutes value, or the time frame involved, short-term versus whole-of-life benefits, so explain. If they agree the returns are sufficient, then the onus is on the prospect to clarify further, "In what way is it too expensive?"

> "Are you saying it is too high, or that you cannot afford it?"

While the price objection sounds good, something embarrassing may be behind it. A willingness to pay and the ability to pay are two very different things and require two very different approaches.

If they can afford it and have the budget, then it is highly likely that they do not see the benefits of what you are offering. It is not price that is the issue, it is value. Focus on their needs, wants and the benefits of your proposal to them. Remember, the more someone wants something, the less they can resist it. Always focus on building buying desire by showing how the specific benefits of what you offer match as well as satisfy their needs and requirements.

Of course, if they cannot afford it, then the question I suggest you ask is, "If you could afford it, would you buy it?" If they say "No," then the issue is not price at all; it is an issue of having not enough desire. So, ask questions to reaffirm their needs and show specifically how your proposition matches them.

If they could afford it and would buy it, then you must explore options around either the budget and how it is allocated, or payments terms that may give more room to manoeuvre.

> "So, to clarify my thinking and consider how best this proposition can represent outstanding value for you, may I summarise what we have agreed to date?"

You are momentarily side-stepping the issue raised. Notice we are using either the word 'agreed' or 'achieved'. This puts a positive slant on the discussion.

By reaffirming their needs and the benefits along with how the benefits match and satisfy those needs, you build up the sense and weight of the consensus between you. The mood becomes one of agreement. You establish how far you have come together. This reaffirms and builds their buying desire. The more they want something, the less they can resist.

This does not answer the objection; instead, you tackle it by demonstrating that any objection now is unnatural when compared to the progress and agreements already made. People prefer to make their next decision in a way that is consistent with their previous decisions. You are suggesting that the journey you have been on together has been positive, full of common intent and goals. You have been on a good run. You have established a valuable momentum between you, and it seems unnatural to stall at this point.

"Let me ask you, are you happy with everything we have looked at?" (Yes) "Are you happy with me?" (Yes) "Our service?" (Yes) "The quality we offer?" (Yes)

This type of approach is called the summary or ascending close. If they *are* happy with everything, then it is valid for you to ask, "Why would you want me to reduce my price?"

Every time you ask a question and they say, "Yes," it is in effect a small close and reduces the opportunity for them to reason and rationalise why they want a discount or to complain about the price.

"Our price is too high?!" (Inflection)

Doing this tends to force them to reveal more about their thinking behind the statement. After all, their price objection could mean any number of things:

- "I haven't got the money."
- "It's more than I thought it would be or can sanction."
- "I'm not convinced of the value."
- "I say that to every salesperson."

What you need is more information. As it stands, you are limited as to what you can do with 'price'. By reflecting it back, the prospect is obliged to give more information as to the real reason behind their initial comment. You are treating 'price' as the skin of the apple. By reflecting the word back with an inflection to turn it into a question, you are taking a bite out of the apple. With more information to orient yourself effectively, you should be able to answer the real concern ethically and effectively.

"What price do you put on getting the results you want?"

"If I may be bold, can you afford not to?"

These questions will not suit everyone. Certainly, it takes a certain kind of prospect and a salesperson with a certain personality type to consider using this mechanism.

These work best when the prospect cannot get the same results from a competitor and pay less. The aim is to establish the scarcity and the extra value in your solution. Fear of loss is greater than the desire for gain, so you introduce the cost of them *not* getting those benefits. "If you were not able to benefit from these results, what would the cost be?" This converts future gain into current pain.

"Let me ask you, if you believed it was worth it, would you go ahead?"

This works well when the prospect says something like, "I got your proposal, but I have to say that it is a lot more than other quotes I have received."

Then the salesperson can ask something like:

"I appreciate that, Mr Prospect, and of course you want to make the right choice. Let me ask you though, if you believed in your own mind that our solution was worth it to you, would you go ahead?"

Logic suggests that the only answer to that is, "Yes," if they have the funds and the authority.

If they say that even if they thought it was worth it, they would not buy it, then they almost certainly have an underlying concern that you do not know about. The only way to find it is to ask more questions.

> "You must have a very good reason for saying that, Mr Prospect; do you mind me asking what it is?"

If they say, "Yes", then you must ask questions to determine what it would take for them to believe it had sufficient value.

Use this mechanism to make sure that you truly understand exactly what the client needs and wants. Defined clearly. Then address those freshly verbalised needs by specifically matching them with elements in your proposal, demonstrating each as you go, if possible. Check for understanding and ask for feedback as you go.

> "Apart from price, Mr Smith, is there anything else that might cause you to hesitate before going ahead with the order?"

This classic trial close is asking for the order subject to their being nothing other than the price. The prospect is forced to reveal:

1. There is nothing else to discuss.

2. There is something else to discuss.

3. Even if there is something else, they are ready to go ahead with the order anyway.

It is a closing question and a qualification question. You are qualifying them as to whether they are ready to buy. You are gauging their buying temperature. Your tone of voice and intent here needs to demonstrate a humble, insatiable curiosity so that the prospect does not perceive you as being too pushy, or too assumptive.

"If price weren't an issue, would you go ahead?"

Clearly, if they say, "Yes," then all you must deal with is how to make it a 'non-issue'. Once they have said that, then it is appropriate to ask more questions to shape and define the basis of how it can be less of an issue.

"What do we need to do to get the go-ahead today?"

"What would you and I have to agree on today for you to feel 100% comfortable with placing the order with us?"

Remember, you are defending your price and by asking questions you are looking for specific justification as to why a price reduction should not be considered. You are asking questions that invite a discussion based on logic and reason, based on fair comparisons, based on what is behind the emotions. Oh no, it is our three Greek friends again: logos, ethos and pathos.

Your questions are an attempt to encourage rational thought, rather than an emotional reaction. While they may feel they deserve a discount or feel that the price is too high, it is generally harder for a prospect to justify logically why you should give a discount.

If they say, "No, price is not an issue and I still don't want to go ahead," of course your problems are a little bit bigger than you were hoping for. Where they mention an alternative proposal specifically you can ask another question.

"Tell me, in what ways is their proposal the same? In what ways is it different? What is missing from one that is included in the other?"

Very few proposals, contrary to what prospects tell us, are the same. Now your in-depth knowledge about your market, your competition, your value proposition and your win statement come to the fore.

> "If someone asked you to cut your prices, when you know you offer an excellent product and service, what would you do?"

Provided this is said the right way, it can lead into a useful discussion. I have on occasion heard the salesperson say, "I guess in your market you must hear the same from your prospects. What do you normally recommend your salespeople to do in such a situation?"

Provided this is not perceived as too pushy, it can get the prospect to reduce their aspirations for a lower price because they are unlikely to do that readily with their prospects. They probably will say, "We normally offer discounts only on bulk purchase, or forward commitments." This then gives you a degree of legitimacy to use whatever they have said they would do, in defence of your own price.

> "Just so I understand, let me ask, if there were no price difference, who would you choose?"

If they say you, then the next question must be, "That is good to hear; please tell me what leads you to that conclusion?" If they say the other company, then I am afraid your problems are bigger than you hoped for. You can still ask the same question though.

In all this, you are trying to get them to reveal that they are comparing your price to someone else's. If not, and you are saying that it *is* your best price, they must come up with reasons why they want you to reduce it.

Around this point, say to the prospect, "I appreciate the need to get the best arrangements and get the most value. Let me ask – is price your *only* criterion in choosing a supplier?"

If they say, "No," then draw out from him the other factors by asking, "Putting price to one side for a minute, how do we stack up in terms of the other criteria?" The clarification of buying criteria could have been done much earlier. Preventing an objection coming up is better and easier than handling one.

As a salesperson, your job is to show them that you are *not* the same as others, while they may try to tell you that you are. Remember your uncommon advantage, which identifies how you offer meaningful added value in ways that your competitors do not. You do not always have to be better – you do always have to be different, or the only difference is price.

When you have fully understood their needs and shown how you are different, through statements that link their needs to features and benefits, then bring the price difference back into the discussion and explain why it is your best price *or* that any difference between you and a competitor is worth that difference.

If he says, "Yes," you say, "I have to be honest with you and say that we don't claim to be the cheapest in our market, in the way I guess that you don't claim to be the cheapest in your market. Yet hundreds of people choose to place orders with us each year for reasons other than price. If your criteria are based *solely* on price and given the fact we are not the cheapest, is it worth us trying on this occasion?"

After attempting whichever mechanism you choose in strategy one to defend and justify your price, then you will be facing one of three outcomes:

1. The prospect is convinced and buys into the reasons for paying your price for the value on offer and so confirms the order.

2. If you feel for commercial reasons that this prospect is a 'nice to have client' but not critical to your business and its growth, stand your ground. This means the prospect either agrees to your original price or you are going to politely walk away. Politely means protecting the relationship itself and keeping the door open for the future. Remember, 'no' means 'not today' rather than 'never'.

   In this case, you are moving to strategy four.

3. If you decide that you *would* like to have this prospect as a customer and are prepared to facilitate a decision in your favour, you are moving to strategy two – negotiate.

If you would like to read more about defending and justifying your prices, visit www.bemoreeffective.com/theprofitsecret and if you are a first-time visitor, register and download the *Defend Your Price Guide*.

CHAPTER 13

Keeping bad weather out: part two

Strategy two – negotiate

In the early 1980s, I worked for the *Daily Mail*. It was a high-pressure sales role driven by daily deadlines and the relentless pressure to fill space in the paper. One Monday there was a push to collectively meet a target of advertising space to be sold by Friday.

Newspaper advertising space was sold by size, measured in column centimetres, back then. On that Monday morning, we agreed the target of column centimetres to be sold by the team and the rate measured in pounds sterling per column centimetre. The exact rate I have long forgotten and is irrelevant to the point. For illustration, let's say the agreed rate was £100 per column centimetre. We were also told that if we had to, we could sell for £95 per column centimetre. Come Friday the space had all been sold, which was a big success, but how much do you think had been sold with the £5 discount?

Over 50% had been sold at the £95 rate. How quickly do you think that rate was offered? Most people had gone down to the £95 by the Tuesday. After only one day. The moment the rate of £100 was challenged by a prospect, even in a mild, curious way, it was dropped. Why? Because we knew we could. The moment an average salesperson believes they have authority to drop prices, such is the urge to close a sale that they will drop the price immediately or show willingness to move.

No wonder that prospects cottoned on long ago to that flaw in our character. That even the mildest push on price can often yield impressive results. The most basic negotiation tactic is never to accept the first price. Another is to use time, information or positional power to create pressure on the other person. How often has a prospect used time pressure on you to squeeze out a discount? How often have you used it to force a decision?

Only after vigorous attempts to defend the price, then, and only then, is the time to consider moving on price. The reasons and situations to consider such a move are best left to you. When you decide it is best to move on price then you deploy strategy number two – negotiate.

Negotiation means trading your concession on the basis that you ask for something in return. Trading is important. No free concessions, even if you could allow it. Trading instead of conceding is part of the Profit Secret.

Get commitment first

Before you start negotiating ask for a commitment, "If I can do something on the price, something that you are happy with and makes sense to my company, will/would you go ahead?"

If is a variable. *Will* or *would* is a commitment. You do not want to do more work on it only to find that the prospect had no intention of giving you the order.

Be sure to establish the fairness point, "…you are happy, and it makes sense to my company…". Most people consider themselves fair. Make the prospect work hard for any movement you choose to make. Some prospects expect you to 'roll over' and concede on price; make it clear that is not you. Give in too easily now and you will train your prospect to expect a discount the next time.

Show you mean business

Having got a commitment, it is best to then say one or a combination of the following:

- "Let me have a think about the best suggestion to help us move forward. May I call you back in an hour or so?"
- "If you are happy with what we come up with, may we go ahead?"
- "Is it still OK to get the decision from you when I call back?"

Calling back to trade

Before calling back, consider what you would like to ask the client for in return. You must get something in return. Fair negotiations are a trade. When you call back, say something like:

> "I have had a good look at the proposal, because you have said you want to do business with us, and we would like to work with you. To help you, I'd like to suggest that by you doing/agreeing to x, I should be able to do z with the price for you."

What you ask for here will vary according to the situation, but could be terms of payment, introduction to a higher authority, letter of reference, bigger order, future order etc.

Trade asymmetrical variables

- **Asymmetrical** means having parts that fail to correspond to one another in shape, size, or arrangement; they lack symmetry.
- **Variable** means being subject to change or adaptation.

In too many negotiations, the trade is over parts of equal value, as in splitting the difference. The salesperson asks for £100 and the prospect offers £50 then one party suggests splitting the difference and the default meaning is to meet in the middle: £75. Fair? Many people think so. Think deeply about this and you realise that both parties lost. They both wanted more. They both gave up £25. This was lose-lose not win-win.

Think about two young children, at home, in the kitchen fighting over a nice big orange. When I say fighting, I mean shouting, wrestling, pulling hair, I mean bad. In walks Mum, sees the fight, works out a quick solution, grabs a knife and cuts the big orange in half. Gives half to one child and half to the other. Problem solved? No, no, both young cherubs turn on Mum, screaming, wrestling – the works. Why? Because they each got only 50% of what they wanted. You see, one child wanted 100% of the flesh to squeeze to make a glass of fresh orange juice and the other was making a cake and needed 100% of the orange peel. Now both had lost. If only Mum had asked a few questions to work out what both children wanted, they could both have enjoyed 100%. Both could have won.

How does that work in business? One of the top companies in Sri Lanka hired me in 2012 to run a two-day negotiation workshop for their senior team. We agreed the £5,000 price plus travel etc. It was a great success. A year later, they asked me back to run the same workshop twice in the same week. My price was £10,000. My contact said, "No way, you taught me to negotiate, the cost cannot be £10,000. I cannot go back to my boss unless I get a discount. I'd look really bad."

I then suggested an asymmetrical variable. "OK, what if I give you a fifth day free. On that fifth day your company runs a public seminar at a nice hotel in the capital. You invite 100 people; they each pay £100 to attend. How much would you generate?" They quickly said, "£10,000 – so the training would be virtually free."

It was agreed to pay me the full asking price, put me up for three more days so I could be a tourist over the weekend, and provide me with the contact details of all the delegates so I could reach out to them as new prospects afterwards. Cleverly, my client put on two seminars, one in the morning and one in the afternoon, each £100 per head, generating enough profit to cover the whole expense of my trip including hotels and flights. What did it cost me? One day? Not really, because I had 200 new prospects and every time I speak at a conference I end up with fresh hot enquiries and almost every time new paying clients. They won and I won.

You trade something of significant value to the prospect that does not cost you anything like the perceived value to them. £1 cannot equal £1 in a trade. I offer you something you value at £50 while that something only costs me £5. We co-design the ideal solution where you get everything you want and so do I. Asymmetrical variables are a brilliant answer in most negotiations, and of course, are part of the Profit Secret.

Essential negotiation rules:

- Be prepared to walk away
- Work out the best alternative to a negotiated settlement before you start
- Listen more than you talk
- Build rapport through everything you say and do
- Ask positive questions that seek detailed explanations
- Summarise your understanding frequently
- Signal a willingness to trade
- Watch for signals of their willingness to trade or concede
- Observe everything that happens and listen carefully
- Record every concession, real or suggested
- Recognise and handle objections as you go
- Keep everything you 'offer' as conditional and your demands fixed
- Keep to your plan and offer for as long as possible
- Any subsequent concession should be half the value of the previous one
- Put your conditions in writing, because psychologically the written word is accepted as less flexible than the spoken word

- Take nothing personally; keep cool

- Be soft on the people and hard on the problem

- Only get passionate about 'what' not 'who'

- Use tactics sparingly

- Use closing techniques throughout

- Learn to handle funny money: smallest possible unit cost – per unit, per minute, per day; or largest – lifetime, total replacement cost

- Focus on interests, not positions

- Remember that the fear of loss is greater than the desire for gain

- Remember that the more need or desire there is, the less resistance

- Never tell another person that they are wrong; find something in what they say that you can empathise with

Negotiating tactics (use sparingly)

While I recommend using these mechanisms sparingly and carefully, some prospects may use them on you. It is an important part of the Profit Secret is to know how to handle the most common. Below are some examples using a car as the item being haggled over.

The flinch. Visual or verbal reaction to any proposal.

Prospect: (Frowns) "Ouch!"

Salesperson: (Small smile) "Oh come on. You have a great car here. Think about x (current pain) and z (wants). Would you rather I showed this car to someone else?"

Nibbling. Attempting to get a little bit more once 'everything' has been agreed. Once the 'decision is made' our defences come down.

Prospect: "That does include a full tank of petrol doesn't it?"

Salesperson: "Oh come on, you have a great price on the car; don't ask me for that as well – fair enough?"

Be prepared to suggest removing previous concessions or extras to stop further demands.

Hot potato. Someone wants to give you their problem. Once accepted, it restricts your options. Test it for validity right away.

Prospect: "I have only £7,000 to spend on my next car."

Salesperson: "That is fine. May I clarify something? If I were to find the perfect car for you, right model, colour and extras, but it would take £8,000, is there any point in showing it to you, or should I show it to one of my other customers instead?"

Higher authority. Someone else, or a decision-making unit, such as a company board, to check with before the final decision enables the separation of negotiations and the decisions.

Prospect: "Thank you for the proposal. I will have to run it past my x next."

Salesperson: "Let's write up the paperwork, subject to x accepting your proposal. They do typically go along with your recommendations, don't they?"

Set aside. When someone says something is non-negotiable.

Prospect: "I will not even look at the new car unless you are willing to give me £10,000 for my current one."

Salesperson: "I know how determined you are to get a good price for your car; I know that is important to you. Let's set that to one side for the moment and explore what else is important to you…" (ask about their pain, needs and desires).

Good guy – bad guy. I like you; I am on your side. I will go and fight this bad guy for you if you will help me.

Prospect: "The board is being particularly tight on expenditure currently. What can you do to help me?"

Salesperson: "That sounds as though you are playing good guy / bad guy with me. If I could find a way to help you, would you go ahead?"

Dumb is smart. I am not a threat to your ego. Be careful, being smart is dumb.

Prospect: "I am not sure of these figures. Could you go over them one more time."

Salesperson: "Yes, I know what you mean; which parts do make sense?"

Now or never. The value of services diminishes rapidly once those services have been performed. If you must give a concession, ask for something in return immediately. Trade!

Prospect: "You can give me a tank of fuel, can't you?"

Salesperson: "OK, if I do that for you, how about you do xxx for me?"

The vice. Squeezing out the negotiating range.

Prospect: "I am sorry; you'll have to do better than that."

Salesperson: "I cannot hit a target I cannot see. Exactly how much better do I have to do?"

Start low. Start low and imply flexibility.

> *Prospect:* "£18,000? I have not had a chance to thoroughly check the car out yet, but my initial reaction is to offer around £6,000."

> *Salesperson:* "How much?!"

> *Prospect:* "Well, what were you thinking of?"

> *Salesperson:* "Let's just set that to one side for the moment and explore what else is important to you" (ask about their pain, needs and desires).

Reluctant buyer. Set up pressure on the other person to concede ground early.

> *Prospect:* "I am not sure we would be interested in it at that price. Just supposing I could interest my x in that, what would be the lowest you could do?"

> *Salesperson:* "Having discussed what you need, and that this car is a good match, I am not sure if there is any room to manoeuvre. You are happy to recommend this car to them, aren't you?"

Favour. Give in this time and I will give you another opportunity later.

> *Prospect:* "I am backed into the corner on this one, with my manager the way he is. Do me a favour, let me have the car for £35,250 and I'll make sure you're given priority to quote for the servicing."

> *Salesperson:* "I am not sure if I could get close to that price. Just supposing I could interest my boss in something near that figure, what else would you be able agree to?"

Win-win or no deal

The above examples can all be used to begin to trade. A negotiation is a trade of asymmetrical variables. A negotiated settlement is not a concession; it produces a win-win outcome.

> **If you want to read more about negotiating more effectively visit www.bemoreeffective.com/theprofitsecret and if you are a first-time visitor, register and download the** *Sales Negotiation Guide.*

Even at this stage you have the right to walk away. If you are not prepared to walk away from an unprofitable deal, or someone not willing to trade, you are only going to lose.

If you decide it is worthwhile to concede, that is strategy three.

To concede or not to concede?

We discussed the true costs of discounts in Chapter 1. If our standard margin is 40%, then with only a 10% discount our gross profit drops to 33.33%. We must now sell 20% more just to stand still. If you currently achieve gross profit of 30% and you decide to drop your price by the same 10%, you will need to do 50% more business to make the same gross profit.

> **If you would like to see the gross profit versus discount table to help you understand the huge negative impact of discounts and concessions, visit www.bemoreeffective.com/theprofitsecrets and if you are a first-time visitor, register and download the** *Discount Table.*

People often say, "Selling on value is fine for some industries. But in my industry, if I do not sell at the lowest price, I lose the sale. It's a competitive, price-driven market." In some cases, they are right and there is not much that can be done about it. In most cases this is a seriously misguided belief. There is a great deal of truth in the observation, "The seller often has more problem with the price than the buyer ever will."

Not surprisingly, companies that compete for business through quotations and tenders tend to have a real paranoia about price. Yet, research by Bonfire into more than 6,600 requests for proposal decisions found that the least expensive proposal won only 10% of the time, while the most expensive proposal won 2.9% of the time.

Of the bids, 90% were won at a higher price and therefore based on something *other than price*. One small business owner I know had this to say about her own perception of price. Joanna is a self-employed physical therapist in Birmingham. She has a small, local practice focusing on helping patients with lack of mobility in the neck, back and shoulders. You may see your thinking in her thinking.

> "I started out on my own many years ago in a very competitive market. As a new entrant to the market, I was very aware of how I was positioning myself in terms of what I offer and my price.

> "I gained many new customers over the years, only to hear their tales of woe that they used to go to another therapist but found they were 'too expensive'. Hearing this certainly reduced my expectations and aspirations for upping my prices, believing that I could only win or keep the business solely on price.

> "After 10 years, I felt that surely a small increase must seem reasonable, if only for increasing costs which to date I had absorbed. I put my prices up by 10% and steadied myself for the exodus of patients. Nearly all my patients said it was about time and because of the superior service they felt it

is worth it. Some mentioned that they could see another therapist for less, while also stating, "I wouldn't get the same treatment." I did not lose even one client. For them, price is not the deciding factor I used to think it was. Now I appreciate that offering an excellent, high-quality service, and differentiating myself with a few things, will almost always be more important than price."

Price is *not* the sole reason that people buy. It is an important element, of course. But providing there is relevant meaningful value, and the buyer is correctly educated about that value, then price becomes less important. It is not so much the price, but effective articulation of the *value* that tips the scales in favour of a sale at a higher price.

That is how the delicatessen survives right next door to a supermarket that sells the same lines at 25% less. That is how BMW and Apple survive against lower priced alternatives. That is how a financial adviser who charges a service fee has more business than they can handle, when their competitors that don't charge are quiet.

What happens if you put your prices up?

I can hear you already. You would lose customers, go out of business and your competitors would have a field day. Check this out. Based on the same 30% margin, if you put your prices up by 10%, you would need to do 25% less business before it affected your true profit. Less work – same profit. Tempting?

Are we in a profession that is losing its edge by discounting heavily on price? Are we losing the fundamental belief that desired value outweighs resistance?

Strategy three – concede

If strategies one and two have failed, you may wish to go to this strategy. I say you *may* wish to use strategy three because you always have the choice to move straight to strategy four.

There may be sound commercial reasons why you feel it appropriate to match a competitor's price or give a discount. There may a bigger picture with a large new account. You may be able to progress on to bigger and more sustainable work. You may be trying to rescue a client who has been slipping away.

It is important to remember that dropping price can send out the wrong signals. It could also signify to the prospect that your price was too high, that you will always do this. They will also expect similar treatment next time. So, what are three key things to consider when using this strategy?

Get commitment first

Like strategy two, always make sure that before you do or say anything, you get a commitment. Ask, "If I can match the price, will you give me the go-ahead now?" You don't want to discount only to find that they had no real intention of giving you the order.

Set expectations

Make the client work by giving you this commitment before you choose to do anything. Make it clear that you do not concede on price all the time. You should be careful here not to set the tone for the next time they come to buy and expect a discount. Say at the very beginning things like:

- "We don't normally do this."
- "I cannot set a precedent. This has to be a one-off."

Be assumptive – take, don't ask for the order

Having got the earlier commitment and set their expectations, it is then time to confirm to them that you will match the price. Now move seamlessly, effortlessly and purposefully on to the details of the order itself. Work and talk on the assumption you are getting the order.

> If you would like the special guide that I've written to help you concede less and hold on to more of your profit, visit www.bemoreeffective.com/theprofitsecret and if you are a first-time visitor, register and download the *To Concede or Not Guide*.

Strategy four – walk away

This is the least preferred strategy. Still, sometimes it is best to walk away while leaving the door open for the future.

Sometimes choosing not to compete in a reverse auction is your best outcome. If you choose to compete on price this time, it may position your company as one that always does – not a good perception to have.

To walk away say something like:

- "I am sorry that we couldn't find a way through this today. While I would like to do business with you, on this project I am going to have to wish you well."

- "Mr Prospect, we are always happy to explore any variation that will provide the optimum benefit to both of us, so if there is anything else we can do to help on this project, please do get in touch."

- "While that may not be the outcome you were hoping for, I would very much hope you will bear us in mind for future projects."

You could even ask them if they have any such projects now.

Leave on a positive note and with a polite tone. After all, neither they nor you can win every time. And this behaviour makes it clear that you prefer win-win or no-deal rather than win-lose.

A business built on the Profit Secret and the value house sales model is one designed to attract the right type of prospect and retain the right type of customers. These are the people who choose to use us for our value-based solutions. These four price protection strategies are also part of the Profit Secret because they will help keep your margins as high as possible. They will help protect your business from the wrong type of customers getting in and from ideal customers getting in for the wrong reasons.

> **If you would like the special guide to help you walk away more appropriately when you have to, visit www.bemoreeffective. com/theprofitsecret and if you are a first-time visitor, register and download the *When and How to Walk Away Guide.***

CHAPTER 14

Future-proofing your profit

After building a house, you, as the owner, would want to protect your asset and increase its value if you can.

Follow through to deliver value

As we said in Chapter 8, follow-up is an often overlooked but important part of the selling process. It is in the best interests of everyone involved for the salesperson to follow up with new customers to ensure that they are 100% happy. Diligent follow-up can also lead to uncovering new needs, additional purchases, testimonials and profitable referrals.

Customer loyalty and retention are part of the Profit Secret

Someone once said that the cheapest business to get is the business you have already got. Now, that means the cheapest cost to you in terms of the cost of a new sale. Acquiring a new customer can cost at least five times more than retaining an existing customer.

Increasing customer retention by 5% can increase profits by 25% or more. The success rate of selling to a customer you already have is 60–70%, while the success rate of selling to a new prospect, for the average salesperson, is 5–20%.

Use the Net Promoter Score® to increase retention and sales

We spoke about the NPS® in an earlier chapter. NPS® can be used as a way to improve customer retention, drive down organisational costs and increase sales. It can help you continually adjust product and service attributes to meet changing customer needs in the most efficient and effective way. How?

1. **Follow up with detractors** (1–6) to reduce customer churn

   To improve your NPS®, you must identify and rectify as many negative customer experiences as possible. Following up with detractors is a good way to identify larger, business-wide issues.

   Send each detractor a personalised follow-up email to address their poor customer experience. The goal is to identify issues that may impact several of your customers and improve the detractor's perception of your brand. Apologise for their experience, ask them for more details and offer an exclusive, personalised package or discount as a goodwill gesture.

   Fix as many of the common issues as you can, then after a short while send a second NPS® questionnaire to those detractors who did take up your exclusive offer, to check for improvements.

2. **Engage the passives** (7–8) to improve retention and sales

   Passives are satisfied customers who will buy from anyone. Almost loyal, just not quite. So, send each passive a survey to ask them what improvements they'd like to see with your product or service, or what issues are preventing them from becoming fans of your brand.

   As they buy from anyone, their order frequency and their average order values are typically much lower than those of your raving fans. Offer them an exclusive discount to increase the survey response rate and explain that the aim is to be able to craft a more personalised solution for them in the future.

Develop as many of the ideas as you can to improve products, service and customer experience. Then after a short while send a second NPS® questionnaire to those passives who did take up your exclusive offer, to assess whether your response led to an improvement.

3. **Involve your promoters** (9–10) in your marketing

   The creator of NPS®, Fred Reichheld, said, "The only path to profitable growth may lie in a company's ability to get its loyal customers to become, in effect, its marketing department."

   Consider each promoter. Think about how each could be a marketing asset for you. What mutually beneficial marketing opportunities could exist? Find common themes to create clusters of promoters who you can approach with the same basic idea. Personalise any communication, rather than sending a standard request to all promoters.

Some things to ask customers to do:

- **Content shares.** Ask customers with an active social media presence to share content on their profiles, linking to your profile or website.

- **Reviews.** Ask customers who praised your product features to write a review on a popular industry review site, linking to your profile or website if allowed.

- **Testimonials.** Ask the best reviewers to write more detailed testimonials on their headed paper or record a short video on their smartphone, or both, with permission to use in your own marketing.

- **Case studies.** Ask those customers with the best value-added examples to participate in writing up a case study with a journalist, with permission to use the materials in your own marketing.

- **Referrals.** Ask all promoters for referrals. More about how later.

In my own experience, the Pareto principle applies: of all promoters, around 20% will be happy to engage with one or more of the ideas above. Appropriate business and personal incentives can be used, with caution, to increase that to nearer 30%.

Promoters are part of the Profit Secret. Imagine you had 100 raving fans, people who promoted you, willingly, selfishly at any and every opportunity. People who spread highly persuasive messages about you for no other reason than they genuinely think you and your products or services are the best. With 100 such raving fans you will have plenty of high-quality hot leads coming your way every week. Most will not ask about price or negotiate and all of them found you; the cost of customer acquisition was in one sense zero. Raving fans are an amazingly powerful mechanism and of course are part of the Profit Secret. Set a goal now to create 100 raving fans.

Testimonials and referrals are part of the Profit Secret

Getting testimonials and referrals is not only simple, it is highly profitable and wonderfully inexpensive. You can find new prospects just by asking peers, associates and existing customers. The lead-closing ratio for non-qualified leads ranges from 5–20% versus a typical 60% closing ratio for referred leads. Customer testimonials are incredibly powerful because the reader or viewer (a prospect) will trust the person in the testimonial far more than they will trust you, especially video testimonials.

Ensure that you have a great two-minute video testimonial for every type of objection you get. Ask your happy client to mention the question or concern they had in mind before deciding to buy as well as some evidence that proves it was a great decision. Then when a prospect raises that objection, invite them to listen to someone else who also brought up that question. Works a treat 97 times out of 100.

The benefits of getting referrals and using testimonials include a shorter sales cycle, higher conversion rates, and a lower customer acquisition cost (CAC).

CAC and CLV are part of the Profit Secret

Use CAC to assess your marketing ROI and optimise your campaigns. Part of the Profit Secret to minimise the cost of acquiring a new customer because that increases your profit margins.

The simplest formula for calculating CAC is:

Marketing and Sales Costs for a period / Number of New Customers Acquired over the same period

Different types of companies have different costs associated with landing new customers. More expensive products and services tend to have a higher CAC. Ideally, you want to recover the cost of acquiring a new customer, whatever the source, within the first 12 months or so.

When you connect with a referred prospect, there will be little time or cost in convincing them because your customer will have already sold your services. This shortens your sales cycle and improves your conversion rate. Testimonials produce similar improvements because with an effective testimonial a previous happy customer's positive words can have three times the weight of your own.

Here comes another part of the Profit Secret. By combining your CAC improvement efforts with your NPS improvement projects you will be increasing your customer lifetime value (CLV). We discussed CLV in Chapter 4.

Most businesses would benefit from driving CLV up while driving CAC down.

The CLV:CAC ratio should be 3:1. In other words, the value of a customer should be three times more than the cost of acquiring them. If the ratio is 1:1, you are spending too much to acquire them or losing them way too early. If it is 5:1, you are spending too little on marketing and you are probably missing out on growth and profit.

It sounds straightforward and it is. You need to know these numbers. Because the more you understand what drives your business, the better the picture you will get of which mechanisms from the Profit Secret you can use more effectively to grow your business.

What has this got to do with referrals?

Simply this. If you design your business or your approach as a salesperson to create a very high proportion of raving fans, your CAC will be low and your NPS high. If you have built profit into each transaction your CLV will also be high. Get the CAC:CLV ratio about right and you will maximise growth and profit. If no one focuses on producing raving fans, then you will have a much harder job to grow as successfully and as profitably. Referrals and testimonials are a Profit Secret.

What is the problem with this approach?

Only that very few business owners or salespeople ask for referrals or testimonials. They get put off by the low 20% success rate, which is a real shame because the 20% who do refer will make a huge difference to any business.

What are the keys to asking?

Trust

The reason referrals and testimonials are so effective is that they carry immediate credibility. Trust is also the key in asking peers, associates and existing customers with whom you have strong and valued relationships; you'll find that if people have sufficient trust in you, they feel safe in handing you something very precious to them – access to their network and use of their name, which potentially puts their personal reputation at risk.

Remember to ask

In 2019, the Sales Insights Lab reported that 57.9% of salespeople ask for fewer than one referral a month. Many people believe that doing a good job is all that is necessary to generate referrals and testimonials. It is not. Even highly satisfied customers rarely volunteer referrals. Get into the habit of asking every satisfied client who benefited from working with you whether they know people who may have the same types of problems they did and may also appreciate your services.

Ask clients who are happy

Going the extra mile can pay off big time. Every time you get positive feedback you have an opportunity to ask for a referral or a testimonial. Not all customers are referral or testimonial candidates. Look at your NPS® 9–10 scorers. Do their networks contain the type of clients you want? If so, ask them for referrals and testimonials.

Overcome the fear of rejection

There is nothing wrong in asking for a referral where you have solved a problem or delivered something of value to your client. Expect around 20% of the people you ask to refer someone. That 20% will make a huge difference to your turnover and profit because over 60% will become customers and a healthy percentage will become highly valuable Pareto customers. So, ask. Ask. Ask.

Flattering egos

Make a big deal about any referral or testimonial received, so that customers know how important it is for your business.

Thinking vertically

The customers of your suppliers, vendors and support services may also want your product or service. Create a reciprocal arrangement. Target complementary businesses that could refer customers to you.

Setting up a system

Include client referrals and testimonials as a seamless part of your marketing plan. Encourage referrals by offering a complimentary gift certificate for services to any client who gives you a referral or testimonial. People will then be able to pass along that gift certificate to people they know themselves.

Here is another part of the Profit Secret. Plant the seed that you want and expect referrals early in the sales process. Then prospects who become clients get comfortable over time with the idea of giving you referrals.

Avoid asking for a referral when presenting an invoice

The conversation that precedes the request for a referral or testimonial is best about the value you have delivered to their business by solving a problem or delivering something ahead of time or above specification. Whenever you can reasonably and appropriately ask about any of those value-adding moments, then is the best time to ask for referrals and testimonials – either or both.

The best time to avoid asking is when presenting the bill.

Referral requests work better face-to-face

People will always be more likely to do something for someone else if the person is standing right in front of them. Unless your normal business relationship is totally, or almost totally over the phone, by email or your website, ask face-to-face, or by video call.

When you ask for a referral ask for a testimonial too

When you are asking for referrals, this is also an excellent time to ask a client for a testimonial: a short, written endorsement or, better still, a short video recorded on a smartphone. These you can use on your website, in brochures or in short success stories you retell verbally to pre-handle objections or explain an advantage of your service.

Not everyone will write or film a testimonial for you on the spot. Some need a template or a short questionnaire or outline guide that they can use to prompt them. If they prefer, you can leave the template with them and ask them to email their thoughts to you.

Ask for a specific introduction

Find out who a customer knows. Do some detective work, check their LinkedIn profile. Where else have they worked? Who has given them a testimonial? Which associations or groups are they a part of? Listen as you get to know them on the journey from prospect to client. Who do they mention in conversation?

You can even start a conversation about the great people they have worked for or met in their profession. Ask them about what they learned from those people. Be authentically curious about those experiences and lessons and they will mention those people by name and will probably tell you where they are now.

When you uncover an ideal prospect for you in their network ask for introductions, not a referral. For example, "Bob, I've wanted to connect with X but haven't had much success. You mentioned working with him previously. Would you be willing to introduce me to him?"

Set a target

Things you measure and review tend to improve, so set a clear goal with a timeline, for example: 10 referrals collected by X. 10 testimonials collected by Y.

Give and receive

Give your clients referrals, extra services and support. When you give willingly to your customers including giving them referrals, they are far more likely return the favour.

Type of customer

Inform your referring clients of the type of customers you can help. Explain to them your ideal prospect profile, as it is likely to provide a clear picture of the customer demographics and characteristics you are looking for. And it is a good test of the profile, because if they do not understand it or recognise people in their network who exhibit similar characteristics then it probably needs rewriting.

Act on the referral quickly

Actions speak louder than words. Prove you wanted the referral and appreciated it. Contact the person that day or as soon as you practically can. And let your customer know that you have acted. Even if you have to leave a message for the referral because they were not available, let your customer know. When you do get to speak to the referral, let your customer know that also.

Send a thank you letter

Treat your referral sources with the utmost of care and you will not only build a foundation of trust but keep hot prospects coming to your door. Thank people in writing by post, make it special somehow, or handwrite it. But please no emails.

Asking more than once

Having trained thousands of salespeople since 1992, my experience is that when a salesperson does ask a client for a referral, they only do that once. It is crazy really when you know that those clients who love you the most are the ones who buy repeatedly. Think about it. If someone gives a referral, you follow it up, you let your customer know and thank them, and 60% of the time the referred person becomes a happy customer. Is it more or less likely that the original customer would refer again? They know how much they can trust you with their network and reputation. Each time you ask and follow through professionally, you enhance your reputation and increase the likelihood of more referrals from the same person.

How do you ask for a testimonial?

Here is a straightforward script that you can improve upon.

You: Mr Customer, would you say you are happy with our products and services?

Client: Yes

You: Feedback is important to us and I would value your opinion on some aspects of our products and services. Would it be OK if I ask you a couple of questions?

Client: Sure

You: Ask some review questions to identify their needs beforehand, the features they liked, the benefits they have enjoyed since and some improvement ideas.

Then say: Thank you very much – that is great feedback. I will talk over your improvement ideas with the team and come back to you.

In the meantime, what you said would be of real value to others who might be considering using us, is it OK to turn my notes into a short testimonial? I will write your comments as if they were a letter from you to me – if that makes sense?

Client: Yes

Underdeveloped customers are part of the Profit Secret

While customers who have been with you for over a year spend 60% more on average than those who are new to your business, they are frequently underdeveloped. They are a great target for you to sell far more at a higher margin than could be easily achieved elsewhere without price resistance. One part of the Profit Secret is to sell more of what you already have to the people you have already got. We discussed account development strategies in Chapter 5.

One of several important strategies mentioned was creating a truth chart, which will help you decide which existing customers have the most potential so are the first ones to focus on.

To find out how to create a truth chart and drive up current customer sales, visit www.bemoreeffective.com/theprofitsecret and if you are a first-time visitor, register and download the *Existing Customer Development Strategy Guide.*

Staying ahead of the buying curve

Here comes another part of the Profit Secret. The right to do business has to be earned and can never be assumed. While you want repeat business, repeatedly and doggedly asking for it can be irritating to clients when it is out of context of their requirements and buying cycle.

To maintain their customer focus, the best salespeople become facilitators, creating a partnership that extends the selling relationship within the customer's company. They realise the need to identify specific needs and then turn their company's products into relevant and highly valuable solutions.

How could you do this?

Holding a series of focus groups

Invite key customers and key prospects to a 90-minute focus group offering them breakfast, lunch or any other suitable incentive. Aim for 10–20 delegates. Fewer is better than more. Organise tables of five guests each with one of your team. Explain that the purpose of inviting them is to understand better the changing needs in their industry. Invite one of them, or a leading industry influencer, to speak on a key topic and pose three or four crucial questions for the table groups to develop answers to. Use a facilitator to guide the discussions about what is important to them, what trends and needs they see as important in the future and what they need from the suppliers to their industry.

Publish the results, at least to the group that came along, as well as those key clients and prospects who did not attend.

You can probably run two or three focus groups over a quarter, provided you invite different people. This will arm you with a wealth of information about what your customers and prospects want. It will also put you in a strong position to win future business, particularly with those that came. You have value-adding ways of staying in touch with prospects and customers that focus on their interests and concerns rather than your desire to sell. You and your company can position yourself as influencers. You can develop products and services that match the trends across your ideal customer groups.

Undertake a survey

This can be done by post or email. It can follow on from the focus groups or pick up on other key topics. You can make it anonymous or not. Make it clear that the reason you are doing it is that you value their opinions about the trends and challenges they see in their industry. Offer a suitable incentive along with providing them with the results of the survey ahead of any wider publication.

Create a short series of questions that can be answered in under 10 minutes, including reading the introduction and any instructions. Be sure to ask both quantitative and qualitative questions. Make sure you ask questions about what defines value for them without mentioning price.

Asking people

Every time you are in contact with customers and prospects alike, whether it is face-to-face or on the telephone, simply weave trend research questions into the conversation at an appropriate time. Use a signpost by saying, "Do you mind if I ask you something?" This will draw attention to your question; then ask a thought-provoking, open question to draw out their opinions. You could weave in some of the questions and answers from previous focus groups and surveys and invite them to add their own thoughts. Make it clear that the reason you are doing it is that you value their opinions about the trends, challenges and value they see in their industry.

Whether you are asking prospects or clients, you are finding out more about your ideal targets. The more you know about their company and the contacts as people, the better. The more you know about what they consider important in terms of the trends and challenges and how they define value, the better.

All this research enables you to make the most relevant and value-adding sales approach.

Feedback is part of the Profit Secret

The one thing we know about change is that it is constant. This is why you need to be sure that as you get feedback from your markets and your customers as they change, you feed that back into your value house sales model. Some feedback may challenge whether you are still approaching things the best way. It may well be that you find out that you *are* doing it in the best way. Consistently successful businesses maintain their success by asking, "How can we do it better?" Feedback is the breakfast of champions. As change happens, as it inevitably does and will continue to do so, it is important that you change and grow accordingly. Change is constant; growth is optional. Choose wisely.

Having regular internal review meetings will help accommodate the feedback about any changes and trends into your business. This regular process will help keep your value house sales approach in tip-top shape and make valuable market information available to your prospects and clients.

Out of any feedback there may be certain messages you want to keep alive internally about the way you do things, or the questions you ask, or the value proposition you offer. Be creative in finding ways to do this including:

- **Staff meetings.** Give someone the responsibility for just one aspect of your value house sales model. For example, at one meeting you could ask one member of staff to consider whether the way you are asking questions and the type of questions is still valid, or whether you should consider adding, deleting or changing any.

- **Screen savers and posters.** Use these to carry reminders of the key messages so your team have them in the front of their minds when dealing with prospects and customers. Change them every month as their power fades quickly.

- **Make sure everyone in the business knows what's happening**, even if they are not directly responsible or involved in certain parts of the process, because there is a huge benefit when people feel included and involved.

If you would like to read more about maximising the value of your current customers, visit www.bemoreeffective.com/ theprofitsecret and if you are a first-time visitor, register and download the *Improving Current Customer Value Guide.*

CHAPTER 15

Conclusion and Covid-19

Will the Profit Secret make my business recession-proof?

The short answer is no and yes.

No, because since the late 19th century there have been more than 255 individual examples of recessions in the Western economies. Of these, 164 lasted just one year and only 32 lasted more than two years. In other words, two-thirds of recessions last for a single year, and only one in eight lasts for more than two years. If we strip out the peculiar circumstances at the end of the two world wars, 70% of all recessions last for just one year.

The conventional wisdom is that the steepness of the fall means that the recession will be a long one, and that the recovery when it happens will be anaemic. Britain has now endured 10 recessions since the Second World War. The early ones in the late 1950s and early 1960s were both short-lived and relatively shallow.

Then, in the early to mid-1970s, an oil price shock helped cause larger contractions in output and a surge in inflation – so-called 'stagflation'. If there were any decade over the past 50 years we'd rather forget, this would be it.

The recession at the start of the 1980s was by far the worst in recent memory. Not only did it last for more than a year, but economic output contracted by nearly 5% – quite a turnaround from the 4% expansion before the winter of discontent took its toll.

Output in the UK fell between 1990 and 1991, but the drop was not as sharp as it had been in the early 1980s; we saw a fall of only 2.5%.

The 2008 crash was one of the greatest jolts to the global financial system in almost a century – it pushed the world's banking system towards the edge of collapse. Within a few weeks in September 2008, Lehman Brothers, one of the world's biggest financial institutions, went bankrupt; £90bn was wiped off the value of

Britain's biggest companies in a single day, and there was even talk of cash machines running empty.

In the short term, there was an enormous bail-out. Governments pumped billions into stricken banks, which averted a complete collapse of the financial system. In the long term, the impact of the crash was enormous: depressed wages, austerity and deep political instability. For 10 years or so, we were still living with the consequences.

In the third week of March 2020, while most of our minds were fixed on surging coronavirus death rates across the world and the apocalyptic scenes in many hospitals, global financial markets came as close to a collapse as they have since September 2008.

Governments around the world were ordering comprehensive lockdowns to contain a lethal pandemic. Built for growth, the global economic machine was being brought to a screeching halt. In 2020, for the first time since the Second World War, production around the world contracted. Never has the global economy suffered a shock of this scale – every country at the same time.

During major crises, we are reminded of the fact that at the heart of the profit-driven, private financial economy is a public institution: the central bank. When financial markets are functioning normally, it remains in the background. But when they threaten to break down, it has the option of stepping forward to act as a lender of last resort. We learned this in 2008 and again in 2020.

The coronavirus pandemic will be a life-changing event for tens of millions of people across the world. When virus infection and death rates stabilise or reduce, and with the financial markets stabilised by central banks, economies, while badly hit, will have a chance to recover.

While no two recessions are alike, most recoveries tend to be consumer-led. Households cut back on spending during a crisis, which creates latent demand; consumers come back, often in a rush, when their outlook improves. Export-led subsectors tend to bounce back faster than those that are not export-led. Because of social distancing requirements, consumers and businesses are shifting to remote channels, and not just in retail. The Covid-19 lockdowns have led to the deepening and broadening of e-commerce and some sectors will never be the same again. Business customers for many kinds of services are having to accept those services will have to be delivered remotely.

So, can the Profit Secret protect my business from a recession?

Yes, because even now salespeople are closing deals around the world, every day, at highly profitable margins. Join them!

The speed of recovery in terms of business and consumer confidence will have a significant impact on the rate at which spending returns. That will be heavily affected by how well the virus is controlled or treated. It will also be affected by the scale of structural change required in any one industry sector. The retail high street shopping experience and low-cost air travel enjoyed in so many parts of the world may never be the same again.

As with any recession, some businesses will simply bounce back; some will have to lean in and learn new ways of working; some will have to restructure their supply chains and delivery channels; and some may not have the cash or the creativity to survive. Many companies that go out of business in the recovery phase after a recession do so because of a lack of cash, or poor operational controls, not because of a lack of gross profit in the sales made at the time. Those businesses may not have been profitable enough before to save a cash reserve to cover a bad spell or invest in the right technology. A crisis does *not* cause the collapse of a business; it merely exposes ineffective mental models, skills and faulty processes that were previously covered up or ignored.

Recessions and recoveries are often cyclical. What we know about recessions is that they tend to force businesses to look closely at costs and overheads. Arguably, this is a time when a salesperson may face more intense price pressure. The question is: are you still trying to win clients with the lowest price, by being the guy who does little favours in a master-slave relationship? Or are you a professional, in an equal partnership with your clients and prospects?

In this economic climate, with harsh competitive waters, building a value house sales model and leveraging every mechanism and principle from the Profit Secret is vital. Despite times being tough, despite there being lots of competition and despite the fact you may be under intense price pressure in your market, millions of sales, deals and agreements are being done every single day around the world where the chosen supplier's price isn't the lowest. In many cases it may even be the highest. Why? Because people (you and I included) simply don't buy the cheapest. As we are all consumers, we will always pay more for something if we think it's worth it.

The best way out of a recession is to sell well and sell often. Do the right things well enough and often enough. This book will help you sell more on value, more at a higher price and more often. This book will move you, your prospects and customers further away from a focus on price.

Remember this definition of selling:

> Selling is the process of enabling someone to discover something of relevant value to them, in a way that is profitable for us.

Every sale you make, and every business, can be built around these three keys: the need, the value and the profit. Profit is the secret that makes sales and business operate authentically. It forces us to become better at creating differentiating value and at explaining how that value more than justifies the cost. That is why profit is the secret to selling more at a higher margin.

Putting the mechanisms and principles from the Profit Secret into place may take an investment of time (what doesn't?). Building your value house sales model properly will be time well spent. As with building a real house, build it properly and you don't have to keep doing major repairs. Yes, you may need to do regular cleaning and the occasional DIY as you would on any house, and that means refining and honing your skills as we have covered in this book. The better you get at implementing the mechanisms and principles in the Profit Secret, the more profit you will make and the more profit you will get to keep.

Acknowledgements

I would like to thank the following companies and individuals for their contributions to this book and their kind permission to reproduce materials in it:

- Results Corporation: True cost of discounting
- Rain Today: Value propositions that sell like crazy
- Robert Middleton: Action Plan Marketing
- Neil Rackham: *Major Account Sales Strategy*
- Robert Bloom: *The Inside Advantage*
- Jim Keenan: The Rise of Social Salespeople
- Jon Katzenbach: *The Wisdom of Teams: Creating the High-Performance Organization*
- Wood & Drolet: How do people adhere to goals when willpower is low?
- Tynan: *Superhuman By Habit*
- Jim Collins: *Good to Great*
- John Whitmore: *Coaching for Performance*
- James Sale: *Mapping Motivation*
- Tim Connor: *91 Mistakes Smart Salespeople Make*
- Jeff Thull: *Mastering the Complex Sale*
- Mahan Khalsa: *Let's Get Real or Let's Not Play*
- Bain & Co: Net Promoter Score

I would also like to acknowledge and thank anyone else that I may have missed out who has contributed to this book.

Permission has been sought to reproduce all contributions and, in most cases, has been received in writing. No request has been refused permission; however, in some cases no response was received.

About the authors

Nick Baldock

Nick Baldock was an international speaker and sales improvement consultant. He had clients across the globe whom he helped become more efficient at converting sales effort into more profitable sales results.

Nick's highly successful sales career, which spanned more than 35 years, started with his selling encyclopaedias door to door. He broke sales records in three industries: finance with American Express; media advertising for the Daily Mail; and recruitment as associate director with James Caan from *Dragons' Den*.

From 1985, Nick delighted audiences across the UK, Europe and the US as a motivational speaker, sales trainer and business development consultant. Organisations such as the Royal Bank of Scotland, SSL International, British Airways, Capital Radio and BMW have testified to the value of his skills and experience. This earned him immense credibility with audiences. With his commanding presence, enthusiasm and sense of humour, he could build a bond with a group very quickly and hold their attention throughout a session.

Nick published his first book, *Running Across America*, in 2000 and his second, *The Value House*, in collaboration with Bob Hayward, in 2011.

On 12 July 2014, not long after completing his third book, *Persuade*, also co-authored with Bob, Nick died unexpectedly of a heart attack. He collapsed suddenly while talking with his wife, Kirsty, and was gone. This was an untimely and tragic finale to the life of a man who had participated in countless marathons, had run 2,851 miles across America, from San Francisco to New York, and had completed two runs from Land's End to John O'Groats – both in under 40 days.

Nick's success stemmed from this simple philosophy: "You can achieve anything, provided you want to."

Half the profits from the sale of this book will go to Nick's daughter, Lauren.

www.bemoreeffective.com

Bob Hayward

Bob Hayward is a Christian, father of four, grandfather of five (so far), Tottenham Hotspur fan and director of two companies, including Be More Effective Ltd, a business growth consultancy.

He has designed and delivered numerous mission-critical internal communication and employee engagement projects for global companies, including Vodafone and the Swedish Bank SEB. Bob has run many skills development programmes across the world. The author of three bestselling books, he is a highly experienced consultant, facilitator, trainer and speaker. Feedback on his work indicates high levels of delegate satisfaction and tangible impacts on business results.

Bob has started seven businesses and built six of them to a turnover of £1m or more. He has a wealth of practical knowledge and experience that makes him a natural and informative speaker with a complete understanding of the needs of employees and problems facing business owners and managers.

Bob met Nick Baldock in 1999, before Nick ran across America. It was the beginning of a profound and special friendship. Nick and Bob hit the national headlines in 2001 when they ran 33 marathons in just 40 days, from Land's End to John O'Groats, in aid of a 12-year-old burns victim, Alfred Page, known as Podge.

Having accomplished this mission, they continued running to raise money for charities that were close to their hearts. They completed a further major test of endurance in October 2005 by running six marathons over six days across one of the hottest places in the world, Death Valley – this time in aid of a charity tackling issues of poverty and deprivation in Swindon. Bob continues to do crazy things to raise awareness and funds for a variety of good causes.

http://www.bemoreeffective.com/

https://www.linkedin.com/in/bobhayward/

https://www.amazon.co.uk/Robert-Hayward